Intelligent Music Teaching

Essays on the Core Principles of Effective Instruction

ROBERT A. DUKE

Center for Music Learning
The University of Texas at Austin

Learning and Behavior Resources • *Austin, Texas*

Intelligent Music Teaching:
Essays on the Core Principles of Effective Instruction

Twenty-fifth Printing July 2020

Published
by
Learning and Behavior Resources
1401 The High Road
Austin, Texas 78746

ISBN 978-0-9771139-0-3

Cover Photos by Judith Jellison

Printed in the United States of America

For Clifford

CONTENTS

PREFACE

This collection of essays is not about how to teach. It's about how to think about teaching and learning. Of course, I'm operating under the assumption that thinking about teaching and learning will ultimately lead to decisions about how to teach, but to skip right to the how-to-teach part without spending considerable time on the thinking part is a big mistake, one that inevitably leads to the kind of unenviable situation in which our discipline often finds itself: hurtling from one "new thing" to another, with little careful thought and critical reflection, becoming mired in contentious arguments over abstractions about which there are little data, arguments that are quite removed from the realities of schools, arguments that seldom bear fruit.

The history of education in America is rife with discoveries and rediscoveries of ideas about how to teach that wax and wane with the passing of decades. But discussions about educational practice that focus primarily on how teachers teach and fail to consider the basic principles of human learning are fundamentally misguided. There is an expansive, rich body of data that illuminates the processes of knowledge acquisition and skill development. Intelligent teaching is predicated on a deep understanding of these processes—how knowledge and skills are acquired, refined, and applied.

How students learn should be the central focus of any discussion about how teachers should teach. Yet, visits to most professional meetings in education reveal a different focus, where much time is devoted to *how-to*... and little attention is given to *why*.... As I observe many conference sessions and workshops that focus on the how-to activities, I am less surprised by a presenter's decision to lead a group of intelligent, musically-literate adults through a series of activities designed for third graders than I am disappointed by the extent to which the session attendees seem to like it. I certainly understand the inherent pleasures of music making, even singing "Six Little Ducks" in a hotel ballroom with 400 other teachers (well, I sort of understand). But to leave the room with nothing more than a new activity for Monday, with no greater understanding of the fundamental principles of human learning that make this activity and others like it an important part of musical development, is to leave the room without having learned anything of lasting value.

This is not how experts think in their disciplines. The systematic study of the nature of expertise has shown repeatedly that experts in all subjects not only possess a vast knowledge, but also organize that knowledge around the "big ideas" of the subject matter. Thus, all the bits of knowledge are connected to other bits, and those bits are connected to form larger principles, of which there are relatively few. These larger principles should be the focus of intelligent discourse in every discipline, including music and music pedagogy.

Precision in Language and Thought

Teaching and Learning

Amble through the corridors of just about any school building in the country and you'll observe teachers and students engaged in a wide variety of activities. One teacher stands on an auditorium stage beside an overhead projector, talking and pointing to images projected on a large screen as listeners scattered throughout the hall write furiously. Another teacher sits at the head of a table in a small conference room leading a discussion. Students seated around the table look through their notes as they raise their hands to volunteer their ideas. Another teacher is seated at a piano in a spacious rehearsal hall, singing and gesturing to a group of young children who stand on risers and sing.

Asked to describe your limited observations, you report that you had witnessed three examples of teaching and learning, a conclusion based on the fact that in each room the person at the front was doing the things that teachers are known to do: talking, explaining, directing, demonstrating. Yes, but how do you know that the students were learning? Well, the students seemed to be attentive; they followed the teachers' directions; they were participating when called on to do so. All true. But is apparent attentiveness an indication that students are learning what teachers are intending to teach? Are there other criteria that should be considered in deciding whether learning is taking place?

9

If you've not thought much about these questions until now, you're not alone. Many people glibly define teaching and learning based on the kinds of surface features described above, all of which pertain to the actions thought to be associated with teachers and students. Is Bill teaching? Sure he is. Just look at him. He's talking and explaining and writing on the board. Teaching. Are Bill's students learning? They seem to be. They're taking notes and raising their hands and volunteering to sing.

In most day-to-day discourse, this cursory way of thinking about teaching and learning is probably adequate. But improving the effectiveness of your own teaching requires that you think more deeply and systematically about teaching and learning. Focusing primarily on the activities in which teachers and students engage without carefully considering the learning that teaching is intended to bring about is decidedly disadvantageous, because teaching and learning are not inextricably linked. Teaching is neither necessary nor sufficient for learning. People can learn without being deliberately taught, and a teacher can inform, instruct, explain, and demonstrate in the presence of students without the students' learning what the teacher intends to teach.

This is an important point to remember as you begin to carefully examine your own teaching: just because you're busy doing things that seem to you like teaching, that's no reason to believe that the students in the room with you are necessarily learning what you intend for them to learn.

Central to understanding anything with an intended function are (1) a clear definition of its purpose and (2) a reliable measure of the extent to which it accomplishes its purported goal. This seems axiomatic with respect to relatively uncomplicated devices like chairs, pencils, potholders, or shoes, and even with respect to more complex systems like automobiles, medicines, communication devices, and skeletal systems. Does the chair comfortably support your body?

Does the pencil produce a fine, smooth line that can be easily erased? Does the antibiotic eradicate undesirable bacteria without harming the host organism? To understand how something works, you must first understand what it's for.

Most professionals are similarly evaluated based on their demonstrations of competence. An auto mechanic's work is evaluated based on whether the car he's charged with repairing runs well once he's finished the job. A trial lawyer's work is evaluated based on his record of winning cases. An investment fund manager is evaluated based on improvements in the health of clients' portfolios.

The evaluation of teachers, instructional programs, and educational institutions seems to be thought of somewhat differently than these other professions. The variables that influence student learning are unimaginably complex, and this fact has led to our avoiding making clear connections between what teachers do and what students learn. Even with the renewed enthusiasm for vaunted measures of accountability at all levels of instruction, the work of individual teachers is usually judged on a range of criteria other than the changes that take place in the students whom they are charged to teach. Instructional programs are often funded, implemented, and retained absent any measure of their effectiveness or, worse, in the face of unassailable data that they do not deliver what they promise. Institutions are most often judged on a variety of indicators that have little to do with the changes in students that come about as a result of having attended the institutions, focusing more on the characteristics of the students who enroll than on the power of the institution to educate its students.

Why is this so? Part of the reason is that the goals of education are seldom stated in sufficient detail to make their assessment possible. Have students learned? Well, it all depends on what you mean by the word "learned," which is tied to the means by which students will demonstrate what they've learned. For our purposes in this and future essays, I define learning as a tangible change in the functional capacity of the learner. In simpler terms: learning is a change in what students demonstrate in terms of knowledge, skills, or attitudes.

Teaching is that which causes learning. Although this may seem rather pedantic and trivial at first, this definition focuses attention on the changes in students that result from learning experiences. Note that this view of teaching does not require a live teacher with intentions, lesson plans, and instructional materials. It encompasses all things that teach, including unstructured, informal experiences that are not specifically designed and have no intentions whatsoever.

For many years the received wisdom in education held that students are like empty vessels into which teachers pour information and skills. In fact, much of teacher preparation is predicated on the presumption that this metaphor accurately captures the teaching-learning process. Nothing could be further from the reality of the situation. Learning is not a passive process. Learning—genuine learning—is an inherently active process that requires some *doing* on the part of the learner. This is not to say that a student who sits and listens to what a teacher says cannot remember the teacher's words and repeat them on command in response to a question posed in class or on a written test. But if this is all that the student can do—repeat an approximation of what the teacher has said in the past—then little has taken place that can be called learning. Learning is more than remembering. Learning requires that the student apply knowledge or skill or both in some meaningful way.

Recent research in science education reveals the inadequacy of many commonly held assumptions about teaching and learning. Students who are assigned a more or less passive role in the classroom may remember much of what the teacher says and does and may be able to repeat this information quite accurately during informal and formal assessments, but the information is very fragile in the sense that it is understood only in the context in which it had been presented. Ask a question in an unfamiliar way—one that requires students to view the information from a perspective other than the one in which it was presented—and poof! the information students had remembered is no longer accessible, no longer useful. Why? Because the students never really understood the ideas presented—understood in the sense that the information was not bound to the context in which it was presented—they merely remembered what they had been told or shown.

Imagine piano lessons in which a student arrives each week at the teacher's studio, and during the lesson the teacher recites important facts about the piano and its history, explains important details about playing the piano, demonstrates playing the piano, and plays recordings of other people playing the piano to provide examples of the literature written for the instrument. The student listens carefully and takes careful notes, but does nothing at the piano. Having observed this kind of activity over several weeks, no one would argue that the student, no matter how attentive and seemingly engaged, was learning to play the piano. Such a claim would seem absurd on its face, because the student never played the piano, and in order to become a pianist, one must actually play the piano.

Now this may seem rather obvious at first, until you begin to broaden the example beyond piano playing to something like "being conversant in the history of Western music" or "understanding mathematics." The measure of a mathematician, music historian, or pianist is how well they *do* mathematics, history, and piano. Each of these disciplines includes intellectual and physical activities that are performed by its practitioners. Mathematicians solve problems, historians document and interpret past events, and pianists play the piano. Of course, mathematicians, historians, and pianists who are considered expert in their disciplines do other things as well, but someone whose understanding of music history was relegated to disconnected bits of information (the birth and death dates of Richard Wagner and J. S. Bach) could hardly be called a historian; just as someone who could only perform calculations could hardly be called a mathematician; just as someone who could play only "Heart and Soul" (even well!) could hardly be called a pianist.

To become a historian, mathematician, or pianist, a student must learn to do things beyond repeating what he's read or been told or been shown. Mathematicians, historians, and pianists perceive and think and act in ways that they have not been taught explicitly. They use the information, gained through listening and watching, to perform tasks associated with their disciplines. And the more active their learning experiences, the more opportunities they have to practice the application of skills as they are learning, the more they will develop the ways of perceiving and thinking and behaving that are the core of expertise.

Think back through your school experiences and you will likely find that most of what you did in school was in response to directives from teachers. Define this word. Read this chapter. Answer this question. Solve this equation. Write this paper. Play this piece. But once school ends, the tasks required of us are not so clearly spelled out by others. We're expected not only to answer questions put to us by others, we're expected to formulate questions ourselves. And, as everyone who is expert at anything knows well, the hard part is not answering the questions; the hard part is knowing which questions to ask in the first place.

And in school, when do students practice that? Well, not nearly as often as they should. In much of our school experience, we answer others' questions, solve others' equations, play others' interpretations. But when the real learning begins, we generate our own questions, apply equations to novel problems, and create our own interpretations. When should this begin? At the very start of instruction. If we want students to learn to become historians, mathematicians, and pianists, then we must have them do the things that historians, mathematicians, and pianists do, right from the start. Now, some may argue that young children and novice adults aren't ready to do those things yet, that they must first master the many prerequisites required for historianship, mathematicianship, and musicianship. Not at all so. In fact, one of the great impediments to students' becoming interested, inspired, and captivated by subject matter is that we generally spend way too much time on these prerequisites—getting them ready for the good stuff—to the extent that many students never get to the good stuff at all.

What's really required before a learner can get to the good stuff? Not nearly as much as many teachers believe.

Learning to teach

It seems somewhat paradoxical that courses about teaching offered by colleges of education often focus more on talking about teaching than on doing teaching. This is problematic, because teaching, like most disciplines, is primarily a doing thing. There is certainly a know-stuff component of teaching expertise, but there is also a very big do-stuff component, and the do-stuff component is where the money is—it's the doing that's most important. But the doing component is harder to learn in many ways, because it requires not only knowledge of facts and ideas, but also practice and refinement of skills, just like learning to play an instrument or learning how to sing. This is one of the most important principles to understand about teaching: teaching is a skill.

Teaching is a skill-based activity that includes a knowledge component and a skills component, but the manifestation of teaching expertise is in the skill of teaching practice—what teachers do. For this reason, it will be necessary for you to reorient your thinking about your evaluations of your own teaching. It seems to me that many students enrolled in teacher preparation classes and practice-teaching experiences view the teaching demonstrations that they perform in class or on videotape as "performances" of a kind. You've been giving class presentations and music performances throughout your school experience, so it's understandable that you would view teaching demonstrations similarly. But that has to change. When you commit yourself to improving the quality of the instruction you provide, you must work to define your teaching experiences as rehearsals rather than performances.

There are certainly many things that you can do to increase the likelihood that your teaching will go well—that your experience and the experiences of your students will be positive—but the teaching itself requires practice. Regardless of how much you plan and prepare, some aspects of your teaching will need to be refined over a period of time. As much as you may prepare for what you intend to do, the fact that you're dealing with live human beings (i.e., students) who will not always do what you expect them to do predicts that you will often have to make so-called in-flight decisions that require some time and practice to master. In fact, much of the "art" of teaching involves dealing effectively with these unanticipated events. Each teaching experience provides an opportunity for you to practice your skills with real, live students.

It takes a great deal of time to develop expertise in teaching. Most estimates in the literature indicate that as many as five years of full-time teaching are necessary to develop teaching expertise, so you need to cut yourself some slack in evaluating what you do now. To expect that every aspect of your teaching will be positive and beautiful right from the start is to expect too much of yourself and to set yourself up to fail. Again, you must learn to think of what you do as rehearsals of your teaching skills rather than teaching performances. I say all of this not to suggest that you lower your expectations about what you aspire to be, but to suggest that you consider carefully how difficult and time consuming it is to develop teaching expertise.

Teaching is a very complicated and messy business. Present in the mix are not only the variables associated with the subject matter that you are trying to teach, but there are the innumerable complexities that are present in every human interaction. Much of the communication that takes place between teachers and students is extremely subtle—so subtle as to be unobserved. This complexity and subtlety are the basis for many people's arguments about the impossibility of teaching people how to teach. "It's an art," they say, "one whose qualities are quite ineffable….Once you begin to talk about the components of teacher-student interactions, you lose the very essence of teaching and have reduced the activity to a series of disconnected trivia." How do you argue with that?

Well, let's begin by considering the fact that any activity performed at its highest level of refinement is at least in some respects artistic. Yo-Yo Ma's performances of the Bach suites, Picasso's *Guernica*, Michael Jordan's play on the basketball court, my mechanic's ability to tune the recalcitrant engine in my Volvo, a doctor's diagnosis of an underlying illness based on a combination of seemingly unrelated symptoms, Wiles' recent solution to Fermat's last theorem. What is it about what all of these people do that makes what they do appear artistic rather than merely algorithmic and pedestrian? It is (1) the simultaneous handling of a great deal of information expressed as many individual variables; (2) understanding the relative importance and contributions of each and the relationships among them; (3) combining the organization of available information with the selection of options from a repertoire of refined and finely tuned skills, (4) one or more of which is then executed with precision. Whew! That's all there is to it.

Now, if you begin to unpack all of that in an effort to understand and explain what's really going on during artistic performance, you may very quickly reach the point where you decide that "it's an art" and leave it at that. It seems unarguable that those who ascribe to the teaching-is-an-art-and-can't-be-taught point of view are correct in their assertion that you cannot provide an algorithmic (i.e., rule-based) procedure that will function positively and lead to a successful outcome in every conceivable circumstance. True enough. There are simply too many variables at work to account for them all with a set of rule-based procedures. But there do exist underlying principles of artistic performance in any realm, and those principles are identifiable, explainable, understandable, and learnable. The hard part, of course, is recognizing how the principles pertain to a given situation and then applying the principles toward the successful accomplishment of goals.

Who are you?

If someone were to ask you to describe the kind of teacher you are or the kind of teacher that you aspire to be, you would probably have some definite ideas about what to say. If you're like most people, your description would comprise a number of adjectives about teachers, like caring, prepared, kind, competent, thorough, conscientious. Most people—teachers, students, and former students alike (i.e., everyone)—hold very similar views about the general characteristics of excellent teachers and the adjectives that best describe them. This remarkable consensus is in evidence throughout the literature in educational research. When asked to describe the characteristics of good teachers, everyone, from educational experts to students themselves, generate lists that contain very similar descriptors.

The adjectives that you use to describe yourself may give some indication of what you think about teaching and what you believe to be important, but they may say very little about the kind of teacher that you actually are. Although you may espouse even strongly held beliefs about the nature of teaching and what it means to be a teacher, the words that you use in speaking and thinking about teaching may not accurately capture who you *are* as a teacher. Why? Because the competence of teachers is embedded in what they do and not in what they say about what they do. Teaching, in essence, is a doing thing. This at first may seem like a distinction without a difference, but as you begin to observe more and more carefully what people say about who they are and compare those observations to what the same people actually do, you will begin to discover the importance of differentiating between descriptions of what people *are like* (nouns and adjectives, mostly) and descriptions of what people *do* (verbs, mostly). This is especially true when it comes to developing competence in highly complex interpersonal skills like teaching.

It is interesting to consider that even those who agree on a subject at the level of broadly stated ideas encounter difficulty when it comes to translating those broadly stated ideas into the specific, doing part. Many of the great debates in education (if there are such things) center on different interpretations of broadly stated ideas. If you were to collect a room full of elementary language arts teachers, for example, all of whom described themselves as "caring," you would probably find those whose teaching more closely reflects the ideals of so-called whole-language instruction and others whose teaching is based on a more traditional, phonics approach. The whole-language teachers, because they are caring, decide not to correct all of their students' written spelling errors in hopes of encouraging students to write freely and confidently. The phonics teachers, because they are caring, make sure that their students spell words correctly in their written work so they can develop a working knowledge of the rules and idiosyncrasies of written English. Even though I'm sure that teachers who practice what they understand to be a whole-language approach and those who practice what they understand to be a phonics approach will see my example as a caricature of both positions, my point is to demonstrate that teachers in both of these groups would describe themselves as caring (the adjectives), but would differ tremendously in their definitions of what caring teachers do about students' misspellings (the verbs).

You've heard sayings like "the devil's in the details," which refer to the differences between broad statements and specifics and communicate the general notion that it's much easier to deal with the big, broadly stated ideas than it is to deal with the specific details that underlie the big ideas. Garnering a consensus about an issue stated in its broadest terms is much easier than coming to agreement about the precise details of what will or what should happen. This disparity between the broad statements and the nitty gritty is what makes political discourse so interesting. "Do you want more freedom and lower taxes?" You bet! "Well, we're going to allow you to manage your own retirement account as we phase out your Social Security benefits." Well, wait a minute!... You get the idea.

The same thing holds true in teaching. Do you want your students to work hard because they're inspired by the intrinsic value of the subject rather than responding to extrinsic rewards or the threat of punishment? Sure. Well, what if, despite your best efforts to inspire, to plan the coolest activities, to explain the inherent value of what you're teaching, some students refuse to work hard or to work at all? Are you willing to wait until they see the light, get inspired, and come around to your way of thinking, or will you decide to intervene with other "motivators," extrinsically speaking? Think about it.

I say all of this to emphasize the importance of explicitness and precision in talking about teaching and learning, because speaking and writing precisely will lead to your *thinking* precisely about what you do as a teacher. The language you use when you speak and write about any experience or idea, not only teaching, will influence the way that you think about it as well. It's very difficult to evaluate your reasoning when it exists only in the privacy of your own skull, and it's usually a simple matter to identify which ideas have not yet been examined outside the confines of your private thoughts. Just try to explain the details of your reasoning aloud. Those ideas that have lived for the most part sequestered inside your head are punctuated with periodic tics like "you know," with the hope that the person who's listening will nod in agreement so you can move on. But the nod, even if forthcoming, should not be interpreted as evidence of agreement, because the listener has not really heard the details of your position, only the most broadly framed aspect of your position. The "you know" is an invitation for the listener to fill in what she believes to be what you think—and as listeners we often do just that—but there is no reason to believe that both you and the listener are thinking the same thing (you know?).

Developing the ability to express yourself in explicit and precise terms will require time and practice, and it may at times seem like more effort than it's worth. But clarifying your language will inevitably change the way that you look at your own teaching and the teaching of others.

It has been well documented across a variety of human perceptions that the words we use to describe what we experience influence our perceptions and our thinking. This is not to say that thinking is necessarily constrained by the limits of language, but it is true that language, perceptions, and thinking interact. The need to make finer discriminations among phenomena and to convey fine discriminations to others requires an expanded repertoire of labels, and learning a repertoire of labels, each of which expresses a subtly different idea, influences thinking and perception. As we speak differently about what we do and what we observe, we think differently, and as we think differently, our perceptions change. The reasons for this are not fully understood, but it is in part attributable to the fact that we are selective in our perceptions of the world around us, and the language we use to talk about what we experience creates expectations, which in turn influence our perceptions.

You know that as a musician you make many more discriminations about the music that you hear than do your friends who have not been afforded extensive experience or formal training in music, and part of what differentiates your perceptions from the perceptions of your less-musically-expert friends is the repertoire of language that you have learned and practiced using over time. Clarinetists make distinctions not only between the timbres of a b-flat clarinet and an e-flat clarinet, but can identify a b-flat clarinet with a "stuffy sound," and can pinpoint the source of the dull timbre as a reed that's too soft. The ability to make such discriminations is not only a result of their having listened to many hours of clarinet sounds. Over the course of clarinetists' experiences, they acquire a repertoire of language with which to describe clarinet tone, and this language interacts with their experiences as discrimination ability develops.

One of the interesting challenges in developing a precise way of speaking and thinking about teaching is the fact that you have been observing teachers and teaching for most of your lives, and this experience, during which you have developed many of your own informal ways of thinking and speaking about teaching, may actually make it more difficult for you to develop a precise language. For most of you, this is your 15th, 16th, or perhaps even your 20th year of formal education. For all of those years, you've been watching teachers teach, at least when you were paying attention, which raises a curious question of why you need to spend more time observing other teachers. Having amassed well over 16,000 hours of teacher observation by this time in your lives, you probably have some definite ideas about what good teaching is and what it's not.

It is true that most people are remarkably reliable in differentiating between good teachers and not-so-good teachers, although reliability (i.e., the level of agreement) among individuals is greater at the not-so-good end of the continuum than it is at the good end. But when it comes to identifying precisely which variables differentiate the not-so-good from the good, and explaining the differences between the good and the really good, reliability falls precipitously, again as a result of the difficulty in expressing the details that underlie the big ideas about which most observers agree.

What you must practice is articulating who you are as a teacher in terms of what you do—in terms of verbs. I think that you will find the development of this skill—speaking and thinking with precision—as gratifying as it is challenging. It promises to change what you notice and what you understand about yourself, your students, and others whose work you observe. Without this skill, it is unlikely if not impossible that you could improve your work as a teacher in a substantive way. It would certainly be impossible for you to evaluate the quality of your teaching and extremely difficult for you to formulate meaningful prescriptions for your students. Verbal precision is the activity through which intellectual precision is developed, and intellectual precision is the linchpin of progress in your development as a teacher.

What to Teach

Goal setting and musicianship

When you meet your students in lessons, classes, and rehearsals, what should be your goals for each session? How will you decide what's most important to teach? And once you've decided what to teach, how will you articulate your instructional goals?

Course objectives typically include the acquisition and refinement of knowledge, skills (including intellectual and physical skills), and attitudes, all of which ultimately contribute to expert behavior in a discipline. You may be surprised to read the word "attitudes" lumped in with knowledge and skills, but attitudes are most certainly a component of effective behavior in physics, geology, philosophy, music, and everything else that we teach in school, although the shaping of attitudes is seldom addressed directly. For now, we'll focus explicitly on knowledge and skills, emphasizing the fact that intellectual skills comprise the application of information in the creation of solutions to knotty problems, the development of plot lines, the weaving together of descriptions that explain political behavior, and the composition of affecting melodies.

Cognitive psychology has long made a distinction between declarative knowledge (knowing stuff) and procedural knowledge (knowing how to do stuff), aspects of knowing that are processed, encoded, stored, and retrieved differently in the brain. The differences between declarative and procedural knowledge are consequential, because the machineries that develop these two categories of competence are not entirely alike.

I think that most people are relatively clear about the dissemination of declarative knowledge. Any individual who's been successful over 16 years of schooling has had to learn how to memorize vast amounts of declarative knowledge—to use the jargon—information that can be expressed in some symbolic form. Facts, algorithms, and recollections of events of the past are examples of declarative knowledge. I *know* that Wallace Stegner authored *Angle of Repose* (declarative knowledge). I know that the force of gravity between two objects is inversely proportional to the square of the distance between them. I know that eating chocolate brings me pleasure. I know the steps required to balance the valences in a chemical formula. I know that *Wellington's Victory* was not Beethoven's best work (it's awful, actually). I know that in 1492 Columbus sailed the ocean blue.

Procedural knowledge, on the other hand, is not generally articulable by those who possess it. I know *how* to ride a bicycle (procedural knowledge), but I can't explain exactly *how* I do it. Although I can skillfully make innumerable adjustments in the position of my limbs and torso to maintain balance and keep the bike upright in the milieu of forces acting upon me and the bicycle, I am quite unable to express in words precisely what it is that I'm doing as I pedal along mindlessly. My knowledge is not, nor has it ever been, expressed symbolically; it is imbedded in my actions. I also know how to play the drums very well, and I can drive a rhythm section in a way that "cooks," but I cannot articulate exactly how I do that—the onset, velocity, and force of each movement of my hands and feet, and the precise relation between the sounds I produce and the sound produced by the bass player. I just try to make the music swing and, usually, it swings. Bench scientists with good hands know how to distribute their time and attention in setting up an experiment, devoting appropriate levels of meticulousness and care to the variables that matter in getting the experiment to work, yet they are unable to explain how they do that either. They just know (procedural knowledge).

The physicist Murray Gell-Mann, when asked about fellow Nobel laureate and physicist Richard Feynman's problem-solving method, described it this way: "You write down the problem. You think very hard. Then you write down the answer." Hmmmm. No one, apparently not even Feynman, could explain how he got to the solution. Genius like that is a marvelous thing to watch. Although it may be very inspiring in a nondirective sort of way, it's not very instructive for aspirants struggling to develop expertise.

In this essay I use the development of music performance skills as a model of procedural skill development, noting that music performance comprises a suite of cognitive and physical skills that are performed in concert to produce artistic expression. You might at first think that this metaphor is too far removed from cognitive development and learning in other domains to be useful, but I believe it is apt because it illustrates some of the fundamental principles about practice and habit strength that are central to cultivating competence.

Often in music performance instruction, goals are expressed in terms of what students will learn to play or sing. For example, "play the b-flat and e-flat scales in two octaves from memory in quarter notes at 120 beats per minute," or "sing *vocalise* number 27," or "play the etude in Lesson 17." Although these are legitimate goals in one sense, they are quite limited in another, and in a very subtle way they focus the attention of both the teacher and the student away from the issue of performance quality and toward the goal of getting through the music.

Note that all of the goals stated above focus on what repertoire students will play or sing, but are silent with regard to how the students will perform any of these scales, exercises, or etudes. By "how" I mean the characteristics that would determine the quality of the performance (e.g., tone quality, accuracy of intonation, rhythmic precision). I should point out that this narrow type of goal setting is very common in music education, where goals for lessons, ensemble rehearsals, even general music classes are typically stated in terms of the activities that will take place during instructional time. Many lesson plans and rehearsal plans that I have examined, even plans written by experienced teachers, list goals like "work on the second strain and the trio of the march" (in a high school rehearsal) or "learn to sing 'Five Fat Turkeys Are We'" (in an elementary music class). I am sure you recognize immediately the gross generality of these statements. What does "work on" mean, exactly? Repeat over and over with the full ensemble until it sounds better? Hear each section play their part alone? Hear individuals play "down the line(!)" for a grade? What does "learn to sing" mean? To be able to sing the correct pitches and rhythms from the beginning to end without stopping? Does intonation matter? Does tone quality matter? Does expressiveness matter (even on "Five Fat Turkeys Are We")? Many teachers would answer yes to these last questions, even when the stated goals about learning to sing the song or working on the march do not reflect this. They certainly do not suggest that the fundamentals of performance quality (i.e., tone, intonation, rhythmic precision, expressiveness) are the primary goals. The learn-to-perform-this-here-piece goals express a different priority, one that focuses most on getting through the music.

You might now be thinking that the way in which the students will play or sing (i.e., the quality of their performance) is implicitly understood: the students should perform these pieces well. But, recalling our previously described quest for precision, this raises the question, What does "play [whatever] well" mean, exactly? After some reflection, many teachers can come no closer than, "You know... well." No, I don't know. Do you know?

The claim that the fundamental goals of performance quality are implicitly understood is false, as evidenced by many teachers' actual instruction during lessons, rehearsals, and classes. If it is true that the fundamental goals are always most important, irrespective of what is articulated in the plan, then we would expect to observe teachers devoting considerable time and attention to these fundamental aspects of performance during rehearsals and classes, and we would expect to hear most of the teachers' verbalizations directed toward the fundamental aspects of performance. But, in fact, we often do not observe this focus of attention, especially during the initial stages of learning repertoire, a new etude, or a new line in a method book. What we often observe are teachers working to get through the piece without stopping but without close attention to the quality of the fundamentals of performance.

Students' views of the world often reflect this getting-through-the-tune way of thinking. We have all heard students claim that they "already know this song" or that they "can already play this piece," by which they mean that they can sing or play most of the notes and rhythms and can perform the piece without stopping. Although their performance leaves much to be desired, in their perception, the piece is learned. But does it sound beautiful? Are the notes in tune? Are the rhythms precise? Is the diction clear? If not, then how in the world did students come to believe that they "already know the piece"? They came to this conclusion because the focus of attention for many days has been on learning the notes and rhythms and words, absent careful attention to the fundamentals of performance.

Naming what's going to be played, sung, or worked on is not equivalent to stating goals. It is merely a statement of what activities will take place during the planned class or rehearsal. The real, long-term goal of developing musicianship in your student is not "to play Line 17" or even "to play Line 17 beautifully." Rather, the real goal, the far-reaching, generalizable goal, is "to play beautifully (period)." The fact that we're playing Line 17 during this lesson is incidental. Line 17 happens to be the stuff that we are using to play beautifully today, but learning Line 17, in the overall scheme of things, is trivial.

This distinction may seem like a lot of ivory tower hair splitting, but the difference between goals that express specifically *what* students are to perform and goals that express *how*, in general, students are to perform are very different and lead to different kinds of instruction. The difference between the *what* goals and the *how* goals is one of the most important in planning instruction in any discipline. This is related to the issue of transfer that I will discuss at length in another essay, but suffice it to say here that the most important and meaningful goals are not those that are limited to the accomplishment of specific, narrowly defined tasks. Rather, the most important and substantive goals are those that have the most far-reaching implications—far-reaching in terms of both time and applicability.

Consider the development of mathematical skills for example. Learning to solve quadratic equations in a particular form, as an end in itself, is a pretty useless accomplishment. Some math teachers may bristle at that statement and may argue that learning to solve quadratic equations is important because it "develops understanding of basic principles of problem solving…" Well, maybe it does and maybe it doesn't. The only way we'll know whether a student's learning to solve quadratic equations has facilitated his "understanding basic principles of problem solving" is to observe the student solving problems other than the ones he's been taught to solve explicitly, not by observing his solving quadratic equations in familiar forms.

All of this is to say that learning an algorithm for solving quadratic equations is not the point, really. In fact, most math teachers would agree that solving quadratic equations, by itself, is not the point, but (and this is a very big but) some would argue that learning to solve quadratic equations *inevitably* contributes to students' skill at problem solving in general. And here's where I, on the basis of considerable data, would vigorously disagree.

If the point of teaching a particular problem solving technique is that students will apply the principles to problems beyond the explicit statements of equations in textbooks or on tests, then there must be specific provisions made not only for teaching students the rules for solving the equations but also provisions for teaching students to *apply* the principles to problems beyond the narrow context in which the principles are first taught. There is a very big difference between learning the algorithm for a particular problem solution and learning how to apply the knowledge and skills involved in solving a particular problem to problem solving in general. The goal of instruction—the real goal, the long-term, far-reaching goal— is not to solve the equations, but to use what you know about solving equations to solve other problems that you may or may not have encountered before.

Similarly in music: learning to play or sing any scale, any exercise, or any piece is never the real goal of music instruction, even though teachers may sometimes verbalize that these are their goals. The real goal—the meaningful, substantive, far-reaching goal—is for students to become superb musicians, doing all of the things that superb musicians do, irrespective of what is being played or sung at the moment. These far-reaching goals for music instruction do not change from lesson to lesson, rehearsal to rehearsal, week to week. The far-reaching goals remain the same *from the first day of instruction* to the time when the student reaches the highest levels of artistic musicianship. In this sense, the goals in the lesson plan never change, regardless of the skill or experience level of the students you're teaching. Only the contexts in which the goals are taught (i.e., the activities, the music) change over time.

Skill-based versus content-based curricula

There's a persistent in-joke about colleges of education, which says that every new competency expected of teachers adds a new three-hour course to the curriculum. Whenever a state legislature in its wisdom decrees that teachers should be competent in dealing with special populations, or reading, or technology, for example, colleges of education respond by adding a three-hour course to their certification requirements. This practice is not unique to education, however. Curricula in most disciplines have traditionally been conceptualized in terms of content; that is, in terms of information to be conveyed to students. As time marches on and the expanse of human knowledge inexorably increases, so does the amount of content in each discipline. I, along with many of my colleagues, have watched with no small measure of disappointment as courses in the so-called liberal arts are crowded out of degrees in the sciences, education, and other professional schools in response to increasing demands for "more content." The education boards of national professional organizations bring increasing pressure to bear on colleges and universities attempting to demonstrate that their students are well prepared according to the dictates of the National Association of Whatever.

This situation is exacerbated by the implicit belief that every important topic in a discipline should have a course with its name on it. As disciplines' subdisciplines expand in size and number, courses commensurately proliferate. Something's got to give way to accommodate all this content. The numbers of hours required for degrees increase, the numbers of electives decrease, and education becomes more and more specialized and compartmentalized.

But this problem is based on a fundamentally erroneous premise, namely, that the core of subject matter expertise is content, a notion that is demonstrably false. Expertise is predicated not on content but on *skills*. This is not to say that content is unimportant. Of course, content is the stuff about which experts think, but it's the thinking and not the content that forms the basis of expertise. Memorizing the periodic table doesn't make one a chemist. It's the use of information about atomic weights and electron shells in understanding the bases of chemical bonds that differentiates chemists from good students who've made good grades on chemistry tests.

Let me say again that I'm not arguing that skills are important and content is not. That's a ridiculous position. But all-content-and-no-intellectual-skills makes Johnny a dim bulb indeed, his ability to name the noble gasses notwithstanding. Seldom are inept students hampered by lack of sufficient content. Although a paucity of facts at one's disposal may be a concomitant deficit in those described as "weak students" or in professionals whose competence is questionable, a lack of information is rarely the root of the problem. No, the heart of most weak students' weaknesses is a lack of skill—intellectual, physical, or social skill.

For a skillful student of any discipline, knowledge is almost always readily accessible. The acquisition of skill, on the other hand, requires consistent, deliberate practice over time. You can't look it up, like declarative knowledge, in the library or on the Internet; you've got to practice it over and over in some systematic way that provides opportunities for feedback and error correction. The development of skills is the meat of learning. The imparting of skills is the meat of teaching, yet, much of students' time in the classroom is spent gathering information, information that is seldom applied in meaningful ways to solve problems, accomplish goals, or illuminate interesting ideas. And much of teachers' time is spent conveying information with the hope that students will eventually put the information to some useful purpose. But hope is not much of an instructional strategy.

Components of musicianship

What are the skills that good musicians demonstrate? Let's consider as an example the fundamental aspects of tone production on an instrument. I include in this category of skills all aspects of tone production and intonation and all of the physical skills that affect tone production. These physical skills include the position of the body; the position of the instrument in relation to the body; the embouchure, the movement of air, the tongue; the holding, positioning, and movement of the bow or sticks on the instrument— every physical component of playing.

Now consider that you, as an accomplished musician, have so consistently practiced the physical aspects of playing your principal instrument that you no longer conceptualize the physiology of playing as a group of individual muscle movements. In fact, many of the subtle variations in the position of your tongue, the shape of your oral cavity, your breathing, and the changes in the shape of your hand on the bow have *never* been thought about explicitly. Some of them you've learned only implicitly through intuition, imitation, and unguided trial and error.

Because instruments and human bodies are constructed in such a way that notes do not all have the same quality and are not all equally in tune, you have learned to make adjustments moment to moment that compensate for the inherent inconsistencies of the tones produced by your instrument. But it is doubtful that you are mindful of all of these adjustments as you play. There now exists for you a single idea that you call "playing position," for example, and although this idea includes the position of your feet, your posterior, your shoulders, your hands, your mouth, your tongue, the position of the instrument…, you think only of playing position and your body seemingly does its thing. Likewise, as you perform a melodic passage, you make countless adjustments in the speed of the airstream, the position and weight of your fingers, the weight and speed of the bow, the shape of your body's insides, all creating the impression that your instrument or voice effortlessly produces consistent, beautifully shaped, homogeneous tones, even though we all recognize that, left to their own devices, our instruments are unwieldy pains in the ass that we skillfully wrestle into submission.

How did this happen? How did you become so adept at performing such complex, multifaceted skills with a minimum of conscious effort? How did you so efficiently turn innumerable muscle movements into unitary constructs? How did feet and distribution of weight and posture and hand position and embouchure all become, simply, playing position?

There is certainly no single thing that one can point to that encompasses all that is playing position. The idea of playing position comprises numerous independent movements that have become so practiced that the independent movements no longer seem separate to you. In fact, your concept of playing position may have become so automatized that it is difficult for you even to remember all of the parts of the whole. It's become something you now just do. The simultaneous execution of all the component motor movements, the monitoring of proprioceptive feedback (i.e., afferent sensory information that lets you know where your body parts are in physical space), and the adjustment of these motor movements during the course of playing have become such a habit that it may be difficult for you to identify and articulate all of its parts, even when you think about it.

In fact, do think about it for a moment, and imagine a single scale, or a line, or an etude, or a piece played beautifully, expressively, and accurately. (Really take a moment to imagine what the playing would sound like, what the musician doing the playing would look like.) Got that aural-visual image? If you do, you're ready to begin to describe in precise terms what you see and hear in your head. And the more precisely you can hear and see the image in your head, the better able you will be to teach whatever it is you're trying to get across to your students.

This example illustrates that many of the ideas that we have in our heads about what musicians do are actually composites of more narrow, specific, component skills. As I've just indicated, playing position involves a constellation of individual muscle movements that work in concert to produce a beautiful tone. Other, seemingly simple ideas like "bringing out the melody" or even "singing more softly" likewise represent constellations of individual component behaviors.

This idea of building composite skills is vitally important, because students learn to produce a beautiful tone, and bring out the melody, and sing more softly by demonstrating the component behaviors that these composite skills comprise. When students experience difficulty in successfully producing a beautiful tone or bringing out the melody or singing softly, it is because one or more of the component behaviors is not in place, which explains why in most cases simply repeating the initial instructions (e.g., "sing more beautifully") often accomplishes little. What's needed instead are instructions and practice opportunities that focus on the successful performance of the component skills of whatever it is we are attempting to bring about.

What musicians do

I've extended this idea to include all aspects of musicianship, and I've printed at the end of this essay a comprehensive list of behaviors that most good musicians demonstrate. The behaviors on the list extend beyond just playing or singing. They encompass all aspects of what musicians may do with music. Please take a few minutes and read through the list when you finish the essay. I know it may seem a bit tedious, but you will benefit from observing the way I've expressed the behaviors that are included. I cannot adequately emphasize the importance of this method of articulating the skills of musicianship.

There are several things I'd like you to notice about the statements on the list. First, note that each line of the document *begins with an action verb*. Each statement thus describes something that an individual does with music knowledge or skill. If we are to learn whether students possess knowledge about music or any other discipline, their knowledge must be expressed in some tangible way. In other words, students must do something to demonstrate the knowledge and skills they possess. And the doing requires a verb. What we know in our heads is invisible to others—and what students know is invisible to teachers—until we express that knowledge in some way, by speaking, writing, or otherwise acting in a way that indicates what we know. Thus you will find no statements below that begin with words like "know," or "understand," or "appreciate," or "hear," or "recognize," or "realize," because all of these words fail to describe actions that can be demonstrated by a learner and observed by a teacher. Does Fred know where the recapitulation begins in the first movement? The only way to find out is to have Fred *do* something (e.g., talk, write, play) to demonstrate that he knows.

Next, notice that each of the behaviors *can be performed by musicians at all levels of experience and expertise*; that is, each item describes a behavior that can be exhibited by beginners and professional musicians alike. This is a very important point. How is it possible that rank beginners and professional level performers could do exactly the same things? Because the *contexts* within which the behaviors are performed vary among levels of competence. By contexts I mean the repertoire, activities, and circumstances in which the behaviors are situated. Look at item I.A.2, for example: "Locates and prepares instrument/materials necessary for rehearsal/performance." Students entering the elementary school cafe-tori-nasium for choir rehearsal, high school band members entering the band room, and members of the Chicago Symphony entering Symphony Hall all demonstrate this behavior. The specific expectations and rules of deportment may vary somewhat among the three settings (though not as much as you might think), but the behaviors are fundamentally the same across levels of expertise.

Consider another example. Item I.B.1.e—"Performs independent part (rhythmic/melodic) with the beat given by the director and performed by other ensemble members"—describes a behavior that is likewise performed by members of the elementary choir, the high school band, and professional orchestra. How can this be? Because the repertoire performed by the elementary choir is much less demanding than that performed by the high school band, whose repertoire is less demanding than that performed by the Chicago Symphony. The point to remember is that performing one's part with the beat given by the conductor is an important component of musicianship irrespective of one's level of skill. All musicians should perform "Five Fat Turkeys Are We," the fight song, and "Festive Overture" "with the beat given by the director and performed by other ensemble members." What changes as musicianship develops over time is not the nature of the skill itself but the technical demands of the contexts in which the skill is demonstrated. Elementary students, high school students, and professional musicians can all demonstrate this skill *at very high levels of competence* if the repertoire at each level permits them to do so. Think about this a lot.

Note also that each of the items on the list at the end of the essay *is one part of a more complex whole.* As accomplished musicians we tend to think more in terms of the complex wholes (e.g., good rhythm) than in terms of the component parts (e.g., synchronizes personal beat with ensemble members), but our students may often need more explicit instruction regarding the component parts. Of course, there will always be students who, when we ask them to "come prepared for rehearsal" or sing "more expressively," actually do what we intend for them to do. But there are many other students for whom the direction to sing more expressively conveys little meaning. These students need more explicit direction regarding the components of responsible musicianship and expressive singing in order to accomplish what we have in mind.

I hasten to add that as students become more and more skilled and knowledgeable, they too will think less and less about the component parts and more about the complex wholes. But at the beginning stages of instruction and when teachers attempt to change fundamental aspects of students' musical skills that are in need of correction, attention must be given to the component parts of the complex wholes. This is not to say that you, as the teacher, must articulate every tidbit and every nuance of every aspect of what you expect your students to do, but it is important that in your own thinking you are able to *identify* the tidbits and nuances that your instructional goals comprise.

Again, you will encounter students who will respond very positively to the broadly stated instructions, like "be a responsible ensemble member" or "sing more *dolce*." But equally often students will not do as you had intended, and it is at this point that you must call upon a deep understanding of the component skills that make up responsibility and expressiveness; that is, you must be able to articulate precisely what your student must do to be more responsible or expressive. The more complex or intractable the problem, or the more recalcitrant the student, the more explicit the required solution.

If you are unable to get much deeper into your definition of "responsible ensemble member" or "expressive singing" than to add more adjectives to your descriptions of responsibility (e.g., dependable, prepared, punctual) or expressiveness (e.g., emotive, expansive, lyrical), then it is unlikely that you will be able to effectively diagnose your students' problems or to prescribe meaningful solutions. You will be left with very few options when students don't respond appropriately, and may resort to simply repeating the same instructions, perhaps more loudly, in the hope that your students will figure out what they actually have to do to accomplish the goal you've set for them, however ill defined the goal may be.

Defining your goals in terms of explicit behavior accomplishes several things. First, it clarifies your own understanding of what you're attempting to teach. Second, it illustrates that many of the ideas that we express in our own thinking and speaking are actually constellations of multiple, component behaviors. Third, it focuses attention on aspects of students' knowledge and skills that are observable, thus focusing not only on what students know and are able to do, but on students' demonstrations of what they know and are able to do. Fourth, it provides a list of component skills that form the basis of musicianship, which is useful both for prescription and assessment of student accomplishment.

Thinking about teaching from a perspective of intellectual precision increases the likelihood that all students will succeed in developing the most important, fundamental skills of independent musicianship. To teach well, we must understand intimately and deeply the principles of our discipline and we must be able to articulate those principles clearly and precisely. We would expect no less from an expert in any discipline. We should expect no less from ourselves.

Components skills of intelligent musicianship

I. Performance Skills

    A. Social Behavior in Music Settings

        1. Enters music room/performance location appropriately

        2. Locates and prepares instrument/materials necessary for rehearsal/performance

        3. Sits/stands in assigned seat/location

        4. Remains quiet while instructions are given or when music is performed by others in rehearsal or performance

5. Raises hand (or gives appropriate cue) and waits to be recognized before asking question
6. Speaks at an appropriate volume level
7. Communicates (verbal/nonverbal) coherently
8. Responds appropriately to verbal instructions—follows directions
9. Responds appropriately to nonverbal cues (visual/ tactile)
10. Works at assigned task as directed
11. Remains stationary while performing/listening to music when appropriate
12. Faces in direction of audience or director throughout performance or rehearsal
13. Moves appropriately while performing/listening to music when directed to do so
14. Sings/plays when given cue
15. Stops singing/playing when given cue

B. Psychomotor Skills/Performance Technique

1. Tempo/Rhythm

    a. Performs successive tones in congruity with a steady pulse
    b. Performs rhythm (melodic) patterns in synchrony with a steady pulse
    c. Coordinates performed beat (rhythmic/melodic patterns) with that given by the director or metronome (aural, tactile, or visual cues)
    d. Synchronizes personal beat with ensemble members (aural cues)
    e. Performs independent part (rhythmic/melodic) with the beat given by the director and performed by other ensemble members
    f. Performs independent part together with different parts performed by others
    g. Maintains initial tempo throughout selection (when appropriate)
    h. Changes tempo appropriately in performance (responds to cue from director)

i. Changes tempo appropriately in performance when applicable (independently creates an expressive effect— rubato, ritardando, etc.)

2. Intonation/Tone Quality/Articulation

   a. Produces resonant, characteristic tone

   b. Adjusts instrument (e.g., slides, joints, mouthpiece, tuning pegs) to match intonation of standard "tuning pitches" (e.g., open strings)

   c. Uses alternate fingerings to improve intonation

   d. Manipulates embouchure and airstream to improve intonation (wind instruments)

   e. Adjusts fingers in left hand to improve intonation (string instruments)

   f. Performs notes with different articulations as appropriate (e.g., slurred, separated, accented)

3. Dynamics/Balance

   a. Performs louder or softer as indicated by the director

   b. Performs louder or softer as indicated in the notation

   c. Selects and performs at appropriate dynamic levels

   d. Performs at a dynamic level that blends with the ensemble or accompaniment

   e. Performs minor variations in loudness to create an expressive effect

4. Wind Instruments

   a. Assumes posture that is erect and relaxed

   b. Inhales appropriately: maximum expansion of body cavity (diaphragmatic and costal expansion)

   c. Exhales with sustained and consistent pressure (abdominal musculature)

   d. Correctly labels the component parts of the instrument (e.g., head joint, barrel, ligature)

   e. Assembles instrument correctly

   f. Performs necessary regular (minor) instrument maintenance (e.g., cleaning, oiling valves, greasing slides and corks)

g. Disassembles and stores instrument correctly, including necessary daily cleaning and storage preparation

h. Supports instrument in a way that allows appropriate embouchure formation and affords relaxed manual operation of all valves and keys (aids such as instrument stands may be appropriate)

i. Sustains long tones

j. Performs successive tones that sound connected by interrupting sustained vibration of lips/reed (airstream) with tongue (i.e., no silence between tones)

k. Manipulates embouchure and airstream to vary the loudness of the tone while maintaining accurate intonation

l. Reed Instruments

  1) Forms embouchure (facial musculature) that allows manipulation of pressure exerted on the reed while allowing the reed to vibrate appropriately

  2) Initiates tone by withdrawing the tongue from the reed

  3) Stops tone with the breath (when appropriate)

  4) Stops tone by placing the tongue on the reed (when appropriate)

  5) Selects and uses reeds effectively

    a) Selects good quality reeds for purchase and use

    b) Prepares reeds for use

    c) Attaches reed to instrument correctly

    d) Performs minor reed adjustments

m. Brass Instruments

  1) Forms embouchure (facial musculature) that allows lips to vibrate freely and creates maximum tonal resonance

  2) Initiates tone by releasing the flow of air with the tongue

  3) Stops tone with the breath (when appropriate)

  4) Stops tone by blocking the airstream with the tongue (when appropriate)

n. Flute

    1) Forms embouchure (facial musculature) that focuses airstream on the back edge of the embouchure plate

    2) Initiates tone by releasing the flow of air with the tongue

    3) Stops tone with the breath (when appropriate)

    4) Stops tone by blocking the airstream with the tongue (when appropriate)

5. String Instruments

    a. Assumes posture that is erect and relaxed

    b. Positions instrument in a way that maximizes relaxation and assures stability of the instrument (violin/viola may use lap positions for pizzicato)

    c. Positions left hand (or right hand, for adapted instruments) with relaxed, curved fingers; using pads of fingers on the fingerboard

    d. Produces tones pizzicato

    e. Holds bow firmly in a way that maximizes relaxation and flexibility of motion (correct bow grip)

    f. Produces tones arco with adequate pressure and speed to produce maximum resonance (full bow and divided bowings)

    g. Draws bow perpendicular to the strings

    h. Maintains consistency of tone when crossing strings

    i. Manipulates speed of the bow, bow pressure, and contact point to vary the loudness and quality of the tone

    j. Performs bowing indicated by written notation or by director

    k. Uses various bowing styles/techniques appropriately to create desired musical effects (articulations)

    l. Selects appropriate bowing pattern in an unfamiliar passage

    m. Correctly labels the component parts of the instrument (e.g., string names, bridge, nut, peg)

    n. Assembles instrument correctly (e.g., end pin, chin rest, shoulder pad, tighten bow hair)

    o. Disassembles and stores instrument correctly, including necessary daily cleaning and storage preparation, loosening bow hair

    p. Performs necessary regular (minor) instrument maintenance (e.g., applying rosin to bow, replacing strings when needed)

6. Percussion Instruments

    a. Assumes posture that is erect and relaxed

    b. Holds sticks/mallets firmly, but in such a way as to allow maximum relaxation and flexibility of motion

    c. Strikes instruments with relaxed, fluid motion that returns the stick or mallet to a position in readiness for the subsequent stroke

    d. Strikes appropriate playing area on each instrument

    e. Manipulates the height of the stick/mallet and speed of the stroke to vary the loudness of the tone

    f. Selects appropriate sticks/mallets/beaters to achieve desired tone on each instrument

    g. Creates sustained effect with rapid single or bounce strokes (rolls); varies the speed of successive strokes to achieve maximum instrument resonance

    h. Correctly labels the component parts of the instruments of the percussion family (e.g., head, rim, tuning lugs, snares)

    i. Obtains and arranges required instruments; assembles stands and frames; positions instruments in such a way as to allow accessibility during performance

    j. Adjusts instruments to achieve desired tone quality (and intonation—timpani)

    k. Correctly performs on a variety of percussion instruments that require idiosyncratic performance techniques (e.g., tambourine, cymbals, maracas, hand drums)

7. Vocal Technique/Tone Quality/Intonation

    a. Assumes posture that is erect and relaxed

    b. Positions head and body in a way that maximizes relaxation and resonance (jaw and lips are relaxed and open)

    c. Inhales appropriately: maximum expansion of body cavity (diaphragmatic and costal expansion)

    d. Exhales with sustained and consistent pressure (abdominal musculature)

  e. Sustains long tones

  f. Controls the use of breath to maintain consistent tonal intensity throughout each phrase

  g. Correctly labels the component parts of the vocal mechanism (e.g., oral cavity, throat, vocal folds, epiglottis) and describes the function of each in singing

  h. Performs successive tones/vowels with consistent tonal quality

  i. Manipulates shape of the oral cavity to maintain the quality of the tone and accurate intonation while singing different vowels (pure vowels, diphthongs)

  j. Manipulates vocal mechanism to improve intonation; adjusts pitch to match tonal center of ensemble or pitch of accompaniment

  k. Produces clearly defined consonants through control of the vocal articulators: lips, jaw, and tongue

  l. Performs voiced consonants that match intonation of subsequent vowels

  m. Maintains tonal focus (i.e., on pitch) throughout performed selection (accompanied/unaccompanied, solo/ensemble)

8. Conducting

  a. Secures attention of ensemble members (e.g., direction of facing, quiet listening)

  b. Gives appropriate conducting signals to members of small/large ensemble (e.g., preparation, begin, end)

  c. Indicates to ensemble members nuances of expressive effect (e.g., crescendo, accelerando, fermata, breath)

C. Music Literacy/Aural Analysis

1. Selects appropriate tempo at which to perform unfamiliar music

2. Identifies notated passages in unfamiliar music that are not immediately interpretable (e.g., rhythm pattern is unfamiliar, unfamiliar notational symbol)

3. Identifies notated passages in unfamiliar music that are technically demanding (e.g., difficult string crossing or large vocal leap)

4. Performs difficult aspects of unfamiliar passage in isolation (e.g., fingering only without blowing or bowing, vocalize rhythm alone while tapping beat)

5. Standard Notation

   a. Correctly identifies the symbols used in standard printed notation (with enlargement, if appropriate) germane to student's performing medium: notes, rests, staff, clef, bar lines, measure, repeat sign, key signature, meter signature, tempo indications (verbal and numerical), dynamic markings, articulation markings

   b. Performs previously unheard selections from standard music notation: plays correct notes in correct rhythmic relationship and with indicated inflection (i.e., dynamics, articulation, tempo)

   c. Correctly notates heard or remembered musical selections

6. Rote Learning/Playing by Ear

   a. Imitates brief rhythmic/melodic fragments performed by the director or heard on recording

   b. Performs brief rhythmic/melodic fragments described by the director (e.g., quarter-note fourth-line D, followed by four eighth-notes: second line G, A, B, C, followed by three quarter notes: fourth line D, second line G, again second line G)

   c. Performs from memory a succession of rhythmic/ melodic fragments (e.g., a simple melody or an entire piece) learned through forward/backward chaining

   d. Operates a tape recorder to record selection to be learned

   e. Operates a tape recorder to locate and play back melodic segments in an order appropriate for memorization

D. Musical Creativity

   1. Improvisation

      a. Creates/performs an original accompaniment to an extant melody

      b. Creates/performs "sound pieces" that employ contrast and repetition

    c. Performs melodic/rhythmic motifs in appropriate tonal/ rhythmic relationship to harmonic/rhythmic accompaniment

    d. Creates/performs original melodies/rhythms that are coherent (i.e., logically consistent organizational structure, clear beginning and ending)

    e. Creates/performs original melodies comprising sequences of melodic motifs in appropriate tonal/rhythmic relationship to harmonic/rhythmic accompaniment

2. Composition

    a. Creates and records (using a coherent notational system) an original accompaniment to an extant melody

    b. Creates and records (using a coherent notational system) "sound pieces" that employ contrast and repetition

    c. Creates and records original melodies/ harmonies/ rhythms comprising sequences of melodic/rhythmic motifs and/or harmonic progressions

    d. Creates and records original melodies/harmonies/ rhythms/ texts that are coherent (i.e., logically consistent organizational structure, clear beginning and ending)

II. Knowledge of Subject Matter

A. Personal Music Repertoire

1. Identifies musical titles, performers/composers of excerpts presented aurally

2. Performs favorite melodies from memory

B. Verbalizing about Music/Music Performance Vocabulary

1. Correctly identifies instruments and voice parts — tone quality (aural presentation)

2. Correctly identifies instruments (visual, tactile presentation)

3. Responds appropriately to formal and informal conventional music terminology used in performance/ rehearsal settings (e.g., solo, *allegro*, from the top, at the bridge, funk, *dolce*, take it out, chorus, soprano, *libretto*)

4. Uses conventional formal and informal music terminology in discussing musical selections performed or heard

5. Uses communicative nonmusic terminology (e.g., analogy and metaphor) in discussing musical selections performed or heard and to describe personal feelings or reactions

C. Musical Styles/Genre, Music History

1. Verbalizes facts about favorite performers or composers (e.g., Paul McCartney was a member of the Beatles; Beethoven began to lose his hearing at the age of 28)

2. Discriminates among contrasting musical styles and among music of different style periods (e.g., be-bop quintet, renaissance motet, romantic symphony, rap group) presented aurally

3. Describes the musical characteristics of (favorite) styles/ genre

4. Identifies style/genre of music presented aurally

D. Music Theory (other than noted above)

1. Correctly identifies melodic motion as ascending, horizontal, or descending

2. Correctly identifies beginnings and endings of musical phrases

3. Correctly identifies the beginnings and endings of harmonic progressions (i.e., harmonic cadences)

4. Correctly identifies harmonic organization of a musical selection (e.g., tonal [major, minor], modal)

5. Correctly identifies chord quality (e.g., major, minor)

6. Correctly identifies harmonic function of chords in context (e.g., tonic, dominant, subdominant)

E. The Music Professions

1. Describes various professional occupations related to music (e.g., recording artist, back-up singer, music therapist)

2. Describes requisite skills and training related to various music professions

III. Music Appreciation

  A. Music Listening

    1. Remains quiet (when appropriate) while listening to live or recorded music

    2. Remains stationary (when appropriate) while listening to music

    3. Moves appropriately while listening to music (e.g., tapping to the beat, dancing) in social settings where movement is acceptable

    4. Operates radio, television, tape, disk, or record players to hear desired music selections

    5. Obtains information about local music events (e.g., concert artists, concert location, ticket information) and broadcast music programming from media advertising or telephone information services

    6. Purchases own tickets and arranges transportation to concert/recital location

    7. Dresses appropriately for the style and genre of concert attended

    8. Attends music event independently

  B. Music Criticism

    1. Selects music to perform that is technically appropriate and personally pleasing

    2. Selects music for personal listening that represents a chosen mood or feeling (determined by student)

    3. Describes reasons for liking/disliking music that is performed or heard using conventional music terminology and/or communicative nonmusic language

ASSESSMENT

What's this doing here?

I'm sure that many readers will find this essay somewhat out of place, appearing near the front of this collection. Most books about teaching deal with issues of assessment at or near the end, an ordinal position that mirrors the perceived chronology of teaching in which assessment and evaluation come into play only after instruction is over. Plan, teach, evaluate, right?

Let's take a moment to rethink this idea. Although it's certainly true that assessment of student learning is often considered a culminating activity, thinking about assessment only in this narrow way is decidedly unproductive.

Many teachers begin teaching without asking and answering the important question of how they'll know that students have learned what they think they've taught. The issue of assessment to some may appear so obvious as to be implicit in any instructional planning, but the extent to which teachers and students continue to be surprised by students' performance on tests, auditions, or juries, or by students' inability to demonstrate what they know in contexts other than those presented to them directly, is ample evidence of the fact that questions of assessment are not tacitly understood. They're tacit all right, but they're not very well understood.

Assessment is inextricably related to the goals of instruction, so the time to begin thinking about assessment is in the planning stages, before instruction actually begins. Implicit in every goal statement is the question of how students will demonstrate that they've accomplished the goal. This is no small point, and it brings into sharp focus the need for precision in our thinking about planning and teaching. How will students demonstrate that they've accomplished the goals we set for them? If we want students to understand key signatures in common practice tertian harmony, for example, how will they show us that they understand?

The current controversies over standardized testing are emblematic of this fundamental question: What should we accept as evidence that students have learned? Ancillary questions that appear often in discussions of public policy are intimately related to this fundamental issue. What should be the criteria for determining the success of a school? How do we know that our education dollars are well spent?

Decompartmentalizing teaching and learning

Most conceptions of education partition teaching practice into curriculum, instruction, and assessment. Teachers are supposed to decide upon their goals, plan how to attain them, and then evaluate whether students learn what's taught. This point of view seems logical enough, until you begin to think more deeply about what all of this means in precise terms.

Even the administrative structures of colleges of education reflect this compartmentalized way of thinking. There are departments of curriculum and instruction that deal with the organization and delivery of subject matter content. This is where the pedagogues live. The psychometricians—the test people—live elsewhere, usually in departments of educational psychology. And although most students of education must take coursework in curriculum, instruction, and assessment, these topics are usually addressed separately by specialists who focus on each apart from the others. Too bad, that. Too bad because what to teach (curriculum), how to teach (instruction), and determining whether students have learned (assessment and evaluation) are not separate at all, but are inextricably interwoven.

Now, many of my colleagues in education will accuse me of creating a straw-man argument, because no one teaching a course in curriculum, instruction, or assessment and evaluation believes that these topics are entirely separate from one another. Of course how one teaches is related to what one teaches, and how and what prompt the question of how well. My concern is that, although acknowledgement of the interrelatedness of ideas may exist in the minds of my colleagues, it is clearly not in the minds of most students, nor does it seem to be a prominent feature in the thinking of many practicing teachers.

It's important at this point to separate assessment, which is a process of gathering information, from feedback and grading, which are forms of conveying the results of assessments to others. This is no small point. Assessment and grading are not synonymous, even though many students, teachers, and principals consider them so. Assessment is "finding out." Feedback and grading are "communicating what you've found out."

Many folks in education go to great lengths to explain how the terms assessment, measurement, and evaluation are different from one another. While it's true that these terms can express subtly different ideas, I find the usual time spent explaining the differences rather pedantic and generally unhelpful. Put most simply: *assessment* is the measurement of a learner's performance; *evaluation* describes the learner's performance in relation to other learners or according to some continuum of graduated labels. "You made 4 out of 28 free-throws (assessment), which stinks (evaluation)."

In this essay I discuss assessment more broadly as a process of data collection—a process of finding out what students know and what they've learned to do. The importance of this perspective is that it emphasizes the finding-out aspect of assessment and illuminates the usefulness of assessment at all points in the instructional process. Assessment is not merely a culminating activity. Assessment is an ongoing activity, one that should be at the fore in a teacher's thinking from the first moments of goal setting and throughout the process of planning and implementing instruction.

The grading issue is another can of worms entirely. Unfortunately, the fact that assessment is often conflated with evaluation and grading leads many teachers to dwell on devising unnecessarily elaborate mechanisms for awarding and revoking points and privileges, computing averages, and converting number scales to letter grades, a process whose complexity convinces other teachers to simply avoid the whole mess for as long as possible. Students, teachers, administrators, and parents who express feelings of anxiety, fear, aversion, frustration, indignation, disgust, or downright hatred toward assessment of learning are for the most part concerned not with the assessments themselves but with the *consequences* of assessment. It's the grades, the test scores, and the audition results, and what those evaluations mean for the future that gets everyone exercised about assessments in school.

This is not an intractable problem, but its solution begins with separating the finding-out aspect of assessment from the consequences of conveying what's been found out in the form of grades, chair placements, admissions decisions, and scholarships. This is no small point, and I invite you to think carefully about your own feelings about assessment, evaluation, and grading from both sides of the grade book, as student and as teacher, and to try to understand the proximate and ultimate causes of your enthusiasm or distress. I too find the grading issue problematic, so I'll avoid the mess for now and will return to the evaluation issues later.

Collecting data

Assessment is data collection, and all of us, whether or not we're teaching, make assessments about what's going on in our environments all the time. We observe the physical features of the spaces in which we move, the sounds that are present, the physical states and reactions of our own bodies, the content of our private thoughts and feelings, and the behavior of others who share our space, all of which we assimilate, synthesize, and interpret to create what seems to us a coherent view of the world in which we find ourselves. Of course, all of this happens without much conscious effort on our parts. Our minds are built to do just this, to receive and interpret the signals in our environment so as to help us formulate decisions about what to do next.

No two people have exactly the same interpretation of a given experience because each of us brings to each new encounter his own history of past experiences, and this history inevitably colors what we see, hear, and feel in the present. Interpretations differ between individuals also because each of us is selective in his perceptions; that is, we tend not to notice all of that which exists in our perceptual fields. There is simply too much to take in at once, and, as a means of accommodating the flood of information that is available to us at any moment, our minds select—sometimes consciously, often not—what seems to be most important and advantageous to attend to. This perceptual selectivity is the combined result of some hard wiring in the human perceptual apparatus and our learning from past experiences, a combination that creates expectations and heightened sensitivities to the world around us.

The combined effects of the hard wiring and experiences are readily exemplified in the development of human language skills. The research data illustrating the perceptual acuity of human infants for speech sounds (and music) are stunning, revealing that infants possess keen sensitivities to sound and are capable of auditory discriminations that most adults would not imagine possible. All healthy infants begin life with the ability to perceive all of the sonic variations in human speech, for example. As infants live and grow in an environment filled with language, their perceptual sensitivities are modified by their experiences, including the relative frequencies of the speech sounds they hear. Human infants learn where words begin and end in the seemingly uninterrupted auditory stream that is human speech, a remarkable feat which they accomplish through comparisons of statistical probabilities of the occurrences of phonemes. Through even the first months of life, infants learn which speech sounds convey information and which do not, and as a consequence they learn to pay attention to the sounds that matter and to ignore the ones that don't. As infants experience the sounds of speech, they learn systematically to attend to sounds that are necessary for understanding, like the difference between the e sounds in bet and beat and to ignore acoustic variations that have no meaning, like the differences in pronunciation among individual speakers.

This learning results in physical changes in the brain that become more or less permanent after the first few years of life. Once the important discriminations are learned, it becomes almost impossible for the child to hear the unimportant variations because the brain has lost the capacity to do so. Thus, the reasons that most non-native speakers cannot learn to speak a language accent-free after the age of six or seven involve not only the speech apparatus but the auditory discrimination apparatus as well. Japanese speakers, for example, find it next to impossible to pronounce r's and l's, and often confuse the two sounds in English. Because the r's and l's of English are not present in Japanese language, but are variants of a single phonemic category, the brain's capacity to make the necessary discriminations between these sounds is lost early in a Japanese speaker's development. It's not only that the lips and tongues of Japanese cannot do the tricks that produce r's and l's, the problem stems from the fact that native Japanese speakers cannot *hear* the difference between r's and l's.

All of this is to illustrate the fact that we are all active data collectors throughout our life experience beginning in infancy, and the data we receive and interpret influences how we think, what we do, and how we feel. This may seem like a trivially obvious observation at first, and only peripherally related to the topic of this essay, but it has profound implications for teaching and learning, since we and our students are collecting and interpreting data all the time. Of course, most of this data collection is informal and unstructured, but it is of consequence nevertheless, because the data that we take in potentially affect what we do, in subtle and not-so-subtle ways.

Assessment in teaching

As we move through each lesson, rehearsal, and class, we make innumerable observations about our students' knowledge, skills, and attitudes. This informal, ongoing assessment guides our decision-making moment to moment as it illuminates the extent to which our students (1) understand what we're talking about, (2) can do what we ask of them, and (3) are interested enough to care one way or the other.

The extent to which we as teachers are consciously aware of the information we assimilate and the extent to which it influences our subsequent behavior varies among individuals and among circumstances. Some teachers are very perceptive about the goings-on in their classrooms and use the information they gather from students to skillfully construct sequences of proximal performance goals, head off problems, elicit student effort and attention, and increase the likelihood that students will successfully accomplish what the teachers have in mind. Others, who fail to recognize the wealth of information available to them, or who fail to interpret the information accurately, are simply unable to explain why students just can't understand what the teacher's trying to put across, or why the students can't do what the teacher asks, *or why they can't just show a little interest! Good grief!*

Of course, a limited ability to size up a situation in which a teacher finds herself is an insurmountable impediment to teaching well, because at the very heart of skillful instruction is the keen perception of what's going on in the room. The education jargon has appropriated the term "with-it-ness" (no, really) to describe this knowing aspect of teaching. Teachers who are said to be with-it know what's going on around them, accurately perceive students' knowledge, skills, and attitudes moment to moment, and incorporate this information into the ongoing process of instruction. Many people engage the same type of skill in informal social settings, company planning meetings, and financial negotiations. These are the folks who are said to be "good with people." Educators and other scholars who buy into Howard Gardner's notion of multiple intelligences would say that these people possess a high degree of interpersonal intelligence. Whatever. The point is that these types of assessment skills are central to successfully leading others to prescribed goals.

The absence of with-it-ness renders effective teaching an impossibility for even the most knowledgeable practitioner of a discipline. The advent of so-called teaching machines in the 1950's was met with optimistic (?) predictions that teachers would soon become less central to the teaching-learning process, if not superfluous, and that students could simply learn from well-programmed instruction absent the intervention of a live teacher. Although the burgeoning sophistication of computer technology has moved the original notion of teaching machines well beyond what anyone could have imagined in 1956, there remains a need for human beings to deliver and guide instruction. Education at the dawn of the 21st century is flush with a dazzling assortment of technological advances, yet we still need human teachers.

What teaching machines then and now lack is the capacity to accurately assess students' knowledge, skills, and attitudes, and to incorporate this information into the ongoing process of instruction *in the moment*, modifying instructional tasks in ways that lead learners to successful conclusions. Now, I'm sure I've just offended some devoted proponents of programmed instruction and CAI, so I hasten to add that I well recognize the fact that current instructional technologies have advanced to a point that their judicious application greatly enhances many learning experiences, but the constraints of computerized instruction inhere in computer programs' limited capacity to accurately interpret the stream of countless data points that human learners exude, and their limited flexibility in formulating reasonable courses of action that incorporate momentary situational variables, IBM's Big Blue's chess victory over Gary Kasparov notwithstanding. Of course, this is, quite remarkably, what human beings do with relative ease all the time.

When teaching is going well, assessment is ongoing. Skillful teachers are collecting assessment data throughout the course of instruction, because the incoming data stream is a necessary component of intelligent decision-making concerning all aspects of teaching: when and how to convey information, assign tasks, and structure learning experiences that develop physical and intellectual skills effectively.

My inclusive view of assessment, which is at variance with many teachers' conceptualizations of assessments as culminating activities, encompasses all opportunities to learn about what students know, feel, and are able to do. Thinking of assessment as an ongoing part of teaching changes many things about how instruction is delivered. I have often heard teachers express that they "wonder how the students are going to do on this next exam." Hmmm. Why do they wonder? Why don't they know? The answer, of course, is that there have been few opportunities for these teachers to observe individual students doing the kinds of tasks that they will be required to do on the examination, so there has been little opportunity to observe whether the students *can* do what will be asked of them when the assessment comes. This is a problem. This is a big problem. If the teacher has had few opportunities to observe students performing the kinds of activities that the assessment comprises, then the students probably have had little opportunity to determine the extent to which they, themselves, are able to perform the kinds of tasks that are on the examination.

A colleague of mine recently expressed a bit of consternation that her students had not performed as well on an exam as she and they had anticipated. Many students in the class had expressed to her that they "understood the material" and were "ready for the test," but they were unhappily mistaken. This raises an important question: What is the dependent measure for determining that one "understands the material" and is "ready for the test"? Now, every conscientious person who's good at anything knows that preparing for something important should include multiple opportunities to practice doing the upcoming important thing, whether that means delivering a paper at a conference, giving a speech, taking an audition, going through an interview, giving a recital. Most of us understand that the more opportunities we have to practice doing the important thing and the more precisely we can anticipate the circumstances surrounding the important thing, the better the important thing is going to go. But students often have much lower thresholds for "understanding" and "ready" than many practicing professionals, not because the students are inherently lazy or apathetic, but because of their inexperience.

Most novices judge the level of their own understanding based on their ability to understand *someone else's* presentation of ideas or to follow *someone else's* instructions to navigate a seemingly impenetrable problem; that is, "If I can understand the teacher's lucid, beautiful presentation of this knotty problem, then I understand it." (Many teachers are smiling right now because they know what's coming next.) OK, so now it's time for the student to explain this idea to someone else. It's test time. No longer following someone else's thinking, the student is now required to generate the linear progression of thought independently, and here is where the breakdown occurs. Because the student has never generated the ideas on her own, because her primary experiences with the ideas have involved only listening to the teacher and the authors of the textbook explain the ideas, because she has thought about the ideas only in the contexts provided by others, she has had virtually no practice in doing what's being asked of her on the test.

I know that this explanation may seem astounding to some teachers, who may think to themselves, "I went over this material so carefully. I took them through all of the issues step by step. I gave them every opportunity to ask questions. I invited them to see me privately for extra help. How could they not understand after all of that?!" Because there were so few instances (perhaps none?) prior to the exam in which the students were required to generate explanations or practice systematically on their own and apply the information and skills in contexts other than the ones in which the material had originally been presented. That's why.

Many novice performers judge the level of their readiness to perform based on their ability to follow *someone else's* instructions to play a difficult passage; that is, "If I can follow the teacher's step-by-step instructions that lead me to a beautiful performance of this clumsy passage today in my lesson, then I can play this." OK, so now it's time for the student to perform the piece on his own in front of an audience. It's jury time. No longer following someone else's beautiful series of successive approximations, the student is now required to perform the piece independently. And again because the student has never performed the passage in this context on his own, because his primary experiences with playing the piece have been under the skillful guidance of his teacher in the studio or alone in a practice room, where stopping to fix mistakes was an inherent part of practicing and where graceful recovery from error was not a focus of attention, he has had virtually no practice in doing what's being asked on the jury.

This is further complicated by the fact that these same novices tend to evaluate their readiness based on their *best* performance trials; that is, their measure of how ready they are to perform is based on their own best performance on their best day under ideal circumstances with little or no pressure. Of course, music performances seldom take place under ideal circumstances and with no pressure. One's readiness is best judged by the extent to which performances go well under circumstances that are as much like the real deal as possible—same performance space, with others listening, with the same the amount of warm-up time, even around the same time of day. Because most performances occur under less-than-ideal circumstances and with some measure of external or self-imposed pressure, having done it once, even really well, should give one little confidence that everything will come together when it's time to walk on stage. Of course, every expert performer understands this fact deeply. We know how many consistently correct repetitions are required before we consider ourselves "ready" for the performance. But many students grossly underestimate what it means to "be ready," and as a result of their under-preparation are often sorely disappointed by faulty performances that they had fully expected to go very well.

All learning requires active practice. Whether the subject matter involves physical skills or intellectual skills, practice is an essential component of developing understanding and skill. No practice, no understanding. As musicians we may think we grasp this better than most, which may be true to some extent, but even we seldom provide the kinds of active practice opportunities in our day-to-day instruction that afford students the practice necessary to internalize what we're attempting to teach them.

Returning to the story of my colleague who was disappointed with her students' test performance, how could she get to the exam and not have a pretty good idea of how everyone was going to do? How could the students be so clueless as to their own level of understanding and readiness for the test? Again, the answer centers on the infrequent opportunities in class to practice generating independent explanations and applying information and skills in novel contexts, all of which were required on the examination.

Now, some of my colleagues may argue that the practice I'm describing is the students' responsibility. After all, isn't that what studying and practicing are all about? That's why we build study spaces and practice rooms. Yes, of course this is what studying and practicing should be about. But if you haven't spent much time lately observing a student studying and practicing, I assure you that doing so will change your perceptions about your students and how they learn. Students need to *learn* to study and practice effectively and independently, but many have not yet learned to do so. I recognize that some teachers see effective studying and practice as volitional issues—if students wanted to study and practice well, they would. I heartily disagree. Students need to learn to study effectively, to practice effectively, to think effectively. So, when and where will they learn that? In class, with us. Not by our *telling* them what to do when they're alone in a practice room or in a carrel in the library, but by our leading them through the very activities that we expect them to do on their own in our absence. In other words, by practicing practicing in our presence.

What I'm suggesting here is that assessment be a part of every rehearsal and every class, that students have opportunities to demonstrate what they know and are able to do independently every time they meet with you. These opportunities need not be elaborate, time consuming, or burdensome, but they should be so frequent as to become a regular part of instruction. This means hearing students play alone in rehearsal (often), having students provide explanations in class (often), having students use the information and skills that they're working to master by applying them in ways that have not been explicitly taught (often).

Most arguments against what I've just recommended concern time constraints and the fear of intimidating students who are put on the spot by having to respond individually. Let's begin with the time issue. First, it is not necessary that every student respond alone every day. You may select students to respond in class based on your perceptions of who can provide a good model for her classmates, who needs opportunities to practice, and whom you need to learn more about. Once you are relieved of the burden of trying to get to every individual every day, this approach seems much more feasible.

Also, students may practice responding in small groups of two to four, which provides many more response opportunities in a given period of class time than is possible if individuals always respond in front of the entire class. Small groups are a multiplier of response opportunities. They provide not only more frequent opportunities for individual responses, they provide students opportunities to react to one another's ideas and evaluate one another's performances.

Regarding the concern that students who are called upon to respond alone in class will be intimidated by the experience: it is certainly true that students who have become accustomed to sitting quietly in class and responding only when they choose to volunteer may be more than a bit frightened by being called upon to explain an idea, solve a problem, or perform a passage alone in front of their classmates. But this fear is almost always a result of the infrequency of their opportunities to do so. If students are left to decide when and under what circumstances they will respond alone in class, many students will understandably opt to stay out of the glare of scrutiny by their classmates and the teacher. But because decisions about when and how often to respond play such an important role in learning, these decisions should not be left to students.

Permitting students to volunteer when they respond alone in class is a fundamentally bad idea, for reasons that are in many ways obvious. Think of who is likely to volunteer. For the most part, those who volunteer are either (1) confident students who are fairly certain that they know the answer or are confident that they can play the passage well, (2) students seeking the attention of the teacher or their classmates, and, most *in*frequently, (3) students who need help. What about students who understand so little that they fail to understand that they fail to understand? What about the students who need more practice opportunities but would rather not volunteer for reasons ranging from fear to apathy? What about the students who can play this passage beautifully but would rather not be singled out? These students and others may seldom if ever volunteer to perform alone or answer a question in class, but there are many important reasons why they should.

A perceptive teacher who's collecting assessment data throughout the course of instruction understands these reasons and how they apply to each of her students. If she is in control of who speaks when, who answers which question, and who plays which passage or which portion of a passage, then the individual response opportunities can be arranged in deliberate ways that provide practice opportunities for those who need them, provide good student models of skilled performance, and provide structured illustrations of systematic error correction that leads to positive conclusions. These and other good reasons for students to respond in class support the notion that the timing of individual response opportunities can and should be under the control of the teacher.

In group instruction, the only way to gather assessment data that accurately reflect individual students' levels of understanding and skill is to observe *individual* students explaining, solving, playing, and singing. I'm often astonished by observing teachers who pose a question to a class, hear the question answered by a single student who volunteers, and proceed along with the lesson as if it has been adequately demonstrated that everyone understands what's going on. But only one student answered. How does the teacher know what the other students know? Of course, the teacher has no idea what the other students know, and the only way to find out is to collect data from the other students. This need not require that every student respond alone every day, nor does it require that students always speak or perform alone in class. Three students can explain an idea to one another in a way that illuminates the misunderstandings that may persist in a learner's thinking. Four students, each of whom is playing or singing a different part, can perform a passage together in a way that affords the students and the teacher a clear indication of who's sharp, who's late, who's out of balance, who's diction is muddy, or whose notes are too short.

Assessment drives instruction

Assessment drives instruction. Maybe it shouldn't. Perhaps it would be better if students, teachers, and the rest of us were not so overly concerned with how we're evaluated. Perhaps. But we are and it does.

Many teachers work to get students' attention off of assessment and on to the subject matter, in the hope of obviating the many questions that teachers hate to hear students ask, questions like "Do we need to know this?" "Will this be on the test?" "How many lines do I have to play?" "How much of this are we responsible for?" Ugh. How did we get to this point? How did students develop such an obsession with their evaluations? Why did they come to believe that the only things deserving their attention and effort are things that will appear on a test or an audition?

The answer of course is that students *learned* to focus attention on evaluations, because in many ways, some of which are actually important, evaluation matters. By that I mean that the results of evaluation often have consequences that affect the future. In professional school admissions, GPAs matter. In scholarship deliberations, SAT and GRE scores matter. In music degree programs, jury grades matter. To many concerned parents, report cards matter. To students who want to sit first-chair, audition results matter.

None of this is inherently problematic. I'm certainly not suggesting that we need to teach students to adopt a cavalier attitude about their grades in school. Not at all. But the problem I wish to address here is that this heightened attention to and concern about important evaluations, for many (most) students, has generalized to *all* evaluations, regardless of their importance or the potential consequences associated with their results.

There are distinct disadvantages to students' being overly concerned with evaluation. First, it places the content of evaluations at the top of students' lists of priorities. What's important? Whatever it is that's going to be evaluated. Now, this would not be such a problem if most evaluations tested the most important, meaningful, and substantive aspects of the discipline studied. But most often this is not what's tested. Most often, tests comprise many disconnected bits of information that "sample a student's knowledge and skills." The problem with the sampling idea is that most tests do not assess whether a learner can actually *apply* what he knows in useful, meaningful ways beyond the contexts in which the knowledge and skills are taught. Most tests require only that students remember and reproduce what they've been told or shown.

"I can define the terms volt, ohm, and ampere." OK, so explain how this electrical circuit works. "….I can define the terms volt, ohm, and ampere."

"I can name which of the 20 amino acids is encoded by each combination of nucleotide triplets." Fine. How does the ribosome translate mRNA into protein? "Did we go over that?"

"I can name the elements of one-point perspective." Terrific. How does the human perceptual apparatus interpret the information on a flat surface as having depth? "Huh?"

"I can name and aurally identify nine different forms that appear in common-practice music of the Western canon: sonata form, rondo form, song form, minuet and trio…." Nice. So, what *is* form, exactly? "Hmmm…."

"I can identify the key name from any key signature." OK, so explain what tonality is. And, now that you know that this piece is in A major, how will that affect how you play the piece? Will you play it differently than you would have if you hadn't known the tonic? *Should* you play it differently now that you know that the tonic is A?

If you've never asked yourself these questions about key before and if you don't have an answer at the ready, then your thinking illustrates the necessity for more careful deliberation about the goals of instruction and the ways we go about evaluating their accomplishment. What *does* knowing the tonic have to do with how one plays a piece? If we can't answer this question beyond saying something like, "You know to play b-flat and e-flat," then we've got a lot more thinking to do, because of course "You know to play b-flat and e-flat" just by looking at the key signature at the beginning of each line. You don't need to identify the tonic to know that. My point here is not that it is unimportant for student musicians to learn to identify tonic keys, but to illustrate the fact that teaching practices and their attendant assessments are not always supported by clearly reasoned rationales.

The greatest problem with most current assessments is that they, the daily activities of instruction, and life beyond the classroom are all so utterly unalike. The obvious solution to this persistent and pervasive aspect of formal assessment is to design activities of daily instruction that more closely resemble life beyond the classroom and to design assessments that more closely resemble the activities of daily instruction. Meaningful assessments focus on what's most important about the discipline, and effective instruction includes frequent opportunities for students to actively practice applying what's learned.

Of course, all of this raises the question of what's important and meaningful, a question that is inextricably bound up with the notion of how learners will use the information and skills in the future, beyond school. Clarifying what's most important and deserving of instructional time begins with our thinking carefully about our expectations for the future. How do we expect learners to use and apply what they know in their lives beyond school? Understand that I'm talking not only about pragmatic applications of knowledge and skills that are work related. I'm referring to using information and skills in all of the ways that intelligent people use information and skills in their interactions with the world around them, at work, certainly, but also at home and at leisure, reading a book, writing a letter, interpreting the newspaper, making decisions about purchasing products, casting an informed vote in an election, making decisions about medical care, singing at a family gathering, reveling in figuring out how something works.

There is a tremendous difference between knowing stuff and applying what you know to accomplish meaningful goals. Being able to solve equations is a good thing, but if it's impossible to connect those equations to anything outside the world of mathematical abstraction, then being able to solve equations is merely academic, in the worst sense of the word, and pretty useless except insofar as it earns good grades on math tests that require nothing more than solving equations. Knowing a wealth of facts about the history of Western music is nice, too, but if one is unable to weave together the events of history to construct a coherent view of the past, then knowledge of those facts can do little other than help score points on music history tests, beat your friends at Trivial Pursuit, and turn you into a bore at parties.

Class piano is perhaps one of the best worst examples of teaching knowledge and skills that seldom progress to their meaningful application. Class piano is a component of music instruction that has the twin disadvantages of being hated by most undergraduates and being mostly unproductive in improving their musicianship. I am seldom surprised by how poorly students who make Cs in class piano play the piano, but I continue to marvel at how poorly students who make As in class piano play the piano. How does this happen? How can students make such good grades and yet be so inept at the very skill the class is purported to teach? Well, because most assessments in class piano test skills that are of little value beyond the class piano exam.

Let's take scales, for example, and begin by asking the question that ought to be asked about anything that's taught, namely, What's the point? The point of scales is to develop fluency, flexibility, strength, and speed in the muscle movements that are required to play an instrument. Scales are exercises in coordination and calisthenics for the mind and for the body parts involved in tone production. And what is required to develop fluency, flexibility, strength, and speed through scales? Consistent, productive repetition of scales; that is, playing scales at speeds that are "fast enough" that the movements begin to become automatized to the point that the player no longer thinks of scales in terms of individual notes, but instead conceptualizes and performs scales and scale fragments as unitary constructs. No longer: note, note, note, cross thumb under, note, note…, but: scale. If a novice can play scales only very slowly, thinking deliberately about each fingering for each note, and that's as fast as she ever gets, then there is *no point* in performing scales. Think about this. A lot.

Of course, the rationale for teaching scales is that they form the basis of the pianist's technique and as such are a requisite part of skill development. So far, so good. But how many of the students in class piano are going to continue to practice their scales after the requirement to do so is no longer present? Will they continue to practice scales until there is in fact a benefit from doing so? For most students in class piano (and you know who you are), the answer to this question is No. Thus, for those people who will not continue to practice scales to the point at which they begin to show a return on the investment of time they require, there is no point in practicing scales other than to pass the exit requirements for the course. (Having read the last sentence, a number of music teachers have hurled this book out the window.) Yes, but students *should* continue to practice scales until they reach a level of proficiency that is advantageous. Yes, but they *don't*. Yes, but they *should*. Yes, but they *don't*. Yes, but they *should*. Yes, *but they don't!*

So now what?

Will this be on the test?

It is undeniably true that assessments have tremendous potential to change behavior. Want to get students to pay more attention to what they're learning? Tell them you're going to give them a test over it. Want to get teachers' attention about what they're teaching? Tell them you're going to give their students a standardized test over it. Want to get administrators' attention about the quality of instruction in their school? Tell them you're going to give their students a standardized test and publish the results in the newspaper. Want to get superintendents' attention about the quality of instruction in their districts? Tell them you're going to give standardized tests and, based on the scores, you will either increase their districts' funding allocations or distribute portions of their extant funding to parents in the form of vouchers, which the parents can apply toward private school tuition.

You get the idea. Give tests. Define the test performance as a contingency for something that matters, and behavior often changes. There are many shopworn adages in education that express this same idea: What's tested is what's taught; assessment drives instruction; etc.

Many teachers and thinkers in education circles bemoan our increasing devotion to test performance as the coin of the realm in education. For many teachers, there is no more insulting pejorative than being accused of "teaching to the test," a phrase that connotes teaching disconnected bits of inert knowledge that contribute little to true understanding. Ouch. Why is this so? Why did "teaching to the test" become a slur to hurl at a disrespected colleague or callous administrator? Why is teaching to the test perceived to be such a bad thing? The answer is that most tests are pretty lousy at measuring a learner's understanding of the most important principles in a discipline. Most tests comprise items that require only that students remember facts or follow algorithmic paths to clear solutions to well-defined problems. But deep understanding requires more than that. Deep understanding involves the application of knowledge and skills in contexts that have not been taught explicitly.

The primary reason that most standardized tests do such a poor job of assessing the application of knowledge and skills in relation to what's most meaningful, interesting, and important about a discipline is that doing so is very expensive in terms of time, effort, and money. Psychometrics is a pretty sophisticated field, and skillful test designers have gotten very good at determining quite reliably and efficiently who knows what and who can do what. In the interest of efficiency and economy, however, most standardized assessments do not require that test takers apply information and skills in realistic (the hip education jargon for this is *authentic*) situations that require more than paper and pencil.

Assessing deeper understanding and the application of knowledge and skills requires a good deal of time and effort on the part of everyone involved: the test designers, the test proctors, the test takers, and the graders. The cost-benefit ratio is a real issue, not only for states considering how to implement a new system of public school accountability, but also for classroom teachers with limited amounts of instructional time.

The extent to which anyone is willing to devote his own time, effort, and energy to assessment is wholly determined by the real or perceived consequences of the assessment. In Texas, for example, regular instruction in grades 3, 4, 5, 6, 7, 8, 9, and 10 *stops* months before the administration of the Texas Assessment of Knowledge and Skills (TAKS), because a school's performance on the TAKS has personal, financial, and political ramifications. Performance on the TAKS *matters*. It matters to superintendents because their districts' publicized ratings of quality and budget allocations depend on it; it matters to principals because their jobs depend on it; it matters to teachers because there are often personal financial incentives to produce high scores; it matters to parents because, well, it's my kid, and, by the way, the value of my property is tied to the reputation of the schools in the district; it matters to students because one cannot receive a diploma without a passing score.

Those who rail against standardized testing as the nemesis of quality education do so not because they object to testing in principle, but because the tests themselves do not effectively measure the application of knowledge and skills in relation to what's most interesting and important about the disciplines tested. Understand that I am not an apologist for critics of standardized tests, and I'm sure that some whom I've lumped into my broad-brush description would disagree with my analysis of their motives. But I doubt that anyone who criticizes the excessive attention to testing and to students' test performance would be nearly as upset if the tests measured something that they felt was meaningful and important about what students know and are able to do. The fact is, unfortunately, that most standardized tests don't measure what's meaningful and important, their reliability and validity coefficients notwithstanding.

Consider an alternative where the tests do in fact measure what's most meaningful and important about the subject matter, in which tests require students to demonstrate the application of knowledge and skills in contexts other than those in which the knowledge and skills were initially taught. While providing a different kind of information to teachers about what students know and are able to do, these tests also convey a different kind of information *to students* in that the test content focuses on what's most important about the discipline.

Of course, just as assessments should embody the most important aspects of a discipline, so should the daily activities of instruction. I'm sure you see where I'm headed here. I'm suggesting that the distinction between the assessments and the substance of instruction day to day should be diminished to the point that the day-to-day activities of instruction closely resemble the assessments themselves. What goes on in class each day? Practicing the application of knowledge and skills that embody the most interesting and important principles in the discipline. What do the assessments comprise? The application of knowledge and skills that embody the most important aspects of the discipline. The assessments closely resemble the day-to-day instructional activities because they all embody the application of the core knowledge and skills in the discipline.

Once the goals for learning have been clearly identified in terms of how students will *demonstrate* what they know and are able to do, the instructional objectives and the assessment criteria have been composed in a single stroke. They are identical. And because these goals focus on the meaningful application of knowledge and skills beyond the contexts in which the skills are explicitly taught, then the daily activities of instruction can closely resemble the assessment activities. Thus, each day's instruction comprises opportunities to practice the meaningful application of knowledge and skills, and these practice opportunities are indistinguishable from the assessments themselves. Now there exists a seamless congruity among the goals, instruction, and assessment, all of which embody the most interesting, important, and meaningful aspects of the discipline. Practicing for the test is indistinguishable from learning the material. Think about this idea for a long while.

A vision of students as accomplished learners

The process of effective instruction begins with designing meaningful assessments, and at the core of meaningful assessment is a vision of students as accomplished learners. Planning, teaching, and evaluating the effectiveness of instruction are all predicated on a clear description of what students will do to demonstrate that they've accomplished the goals set out for them. At the end of a given period of instruction—a day, a chapter, a unit, a six-weeks, a semester, a degree program—what do you expect your students to be like? What must they do to provide clear and convincing evidence of their competence?

The more vividly we can envision an exemplary student who has successfully accomplished the goals we set out, the more intelligently we can organize our instructional time and activities to facilitate the accomplishment of those goals by all of our students. This vivid image of students as accomplished learners at once defines the goals for instruction, the assessment criteria, and the substance of instructional activities, because the goals/assessments define how students will demonstrate their understanding and skills, and the instructional activities will be composed of structured opportunities to practice the goals/assessments.

There is no more effective means of providing structure, hierarchy, and priority to instruction than by composing the assessments before instruction begins. By this I mean actually sitting down before the start of the semester and writing the final exam or designing the culminating project assignment. The final exam defines the syllabus, because the final exam represents the embodiment of what you believe to be the most important goals of your class.

Teaching for the test in this way is entirely appropriate, because the test embodies what we care about most. The test is the tangible expression of the goals, which describe the *application* of knowledge and skills. Every superb teacher has a clear, vivid image of her students as accomplished, competent learners, engaging in the types of activities that closely resemble those that are likely to occur beyond school.

SONGLEADING PERFORMANCE CHECKLIST

Performance #:   Date:

Guitarist: Score (.5 for each YES):

Song Title:

YES	NO	Posture: Sat up straight
YES	NO	Posture: Guitar in vertical plane
YES	NO	Began immediately when called upon (no nervous mannerisms)
YES	NO	Smiled
YES	NO	Gave correct starting pitch
YES	NO	Played appropriate introduction
YES	NO	Introduction in same tempo as song
YES	NO	Cued singers (e.g., "Ready, sing")
YES	NO	Looked at singers at start of song
YES	NO	Looked at singers at least twice during song
YES	NO	Looked at singers at end of song
YES	NO	Sang with singers during song (audibly and in tune)
YES	NO	Played correct chords
YES	NO	All strings vibrate with clear tone
YES	NO	Changed chords without pause
YES	NO N/A	If missed chord, continued without pause
YES	NO	Used appropriate right hand pattern
YES	NO	Played appropriate bass strings (strum or pluck)
YES	NO	Maintained steady pulse in right hand
YES	NO	Played loudly enough to be heard throughout

New Left Hand Technique or Chord:

New Right Hand Technique:

Specify positive aspects of this performance (at least four):

Specify one goal for improvement:

This evaluation accurately reflects the performance reviewed:

                    _____

                      (Signature)

The fundamental principles that form the basis of intelligent assessment can perhaps best be conveyed through an example. Pictured above is a checklist I use for evaluating guitar playing and song leading. I adapted this checklist some 20 years ago from a dissertation project conducted by a graduate school classmate of mine.* Look it over for a minute or so and consider carefully the items on the list. Note that the checklist comprises 20 verb phrases, which, taken together, outline what a confident, competent, guitar-playing song leader does when she's performing well. The composite of all the individual items is essentially a concise description of a confident, competent, guitar-playing song leader in action. If guitar-playing song leaders do everything on the list, they look and sound pretty good.

How was the list generated? By beginning with *a vision of students as accomplished learners*—which in this case means a vivid image of a competent, confident, guitar-playing song leader—and constructing a clear and concise description of what that competent, confident, guitar-playing song leader looks and sounds like. The resulting list comprises all of the essential components of good guitar playing and song leading.

Note that the checklist does not define the difficulty level of the piece performed. In this sense it is context-independent, because the skills described on the list are applicable whether the performer being evaluated is playing his first two-chord song or is the opening act for Asleep at the Wheel. All competent, confident, guitar-playing song leaders do (or should do) all of the things on the list every time they play, throughout their musical journeys from novice to expert. Using a single list to describe the fundamental skills of musicianship, or any other skill for that matter, over an entire course of study recognizes that skill acquisition is a process of developing habit strength through consistent, productive repetition over time.

---

*Furman, C. E. (1985). *Behavior checklists and videotapes versus standard instructor feedback in the development of a music teaching competency.* Unpublished doctoral dissertation, The Florida State University.

Nor does the assessment include scaled ratings for each of the variables on the list. Instead, each item is assessed with a dichotomous Yes or No. I will explain this briefly here only by saying that applying an evaluation scale to each item on the list unnecessarily complicates the assessment and provides no useful information for the students. Making judgments about what rating to assign requires time and thought but contributes little of value. "Well, he sort of smiled and he played most of the chords, and he only paused once." So, out of a possible 5 points for each item, is that a 2 and a 4 and a 3? If it is, what does the average mean? Is it to be interpreted as an overall score? Is this a reasonable estimation of the performer's skills? You see the growing complication here, a complication that brings the added disadvantage of being pretty useless, except as a basis for arguing about grades.

But shouldn't the student who played most of the correct chords get some credit for that? Does missing one chord really warrant a No? Well, the student didn't play the correct chords, so a No for Played Correct Chords is appropriate in this case. The reason it's appropriate to assign a No to someone who missed only one chord is that Played Correct Chords is only 1 of 20 criteria, and it contributes only 1/20th of the student's score. The effect of missing any one criterion is of little consequence in terms of the student's grade, because the relative weight of each aspect of performance is built into the assessment criteria.

Note some of the important principles at work in this approach to assessment. The first is that students know at the outset (1) what is important about what they're learning, (2) what is expected of them in terms of their own performance, and (3) how their meeting these expectations will contribute to their grade in the course.

The second point is that the assessment criteria remain the same throughout the course of study. Why? Because the assessment criteria are not based on course content (in this case, repertoire), but are based on the application of intellectual and physical skills. The fundamental skills don't change as one becomes more and more expert in a discipline, but the contexts (repertoire) in which the skills are applied become more and more sophisticated and demanding.

The third important point about this form of assessment is that the assessment criteria focus on the application of knowledge and skills in context—in particular, in a context that is very much like the extracurricular contexts in which the knowledge and skills are likely to be applied long after the course is over.

The fourth point is that the items are constructed so as to apportion weight appropriately, and as a result the students are less likely to ascribe undue importance to aspects of their performance that are not as consequential as they might be perceived to be by a novice.

The fifth point is that the context for the assessment requires students to demonstrate all of the skills on the list from the very beginning of their experience as learners. Of course, it's no big deal to smile (at least for most), begin immediately when called upon, sing loudly enough to be heard, or use the appropriate bass strings. The hard part is doing all of these things at the same time while you're performing in front of your peers and your teacher. And it's the inability to apply multiple skills simultaneously that keeps people from becoming confident, competent, guitar-playing song leaders, excellent point guards, successful personnel managers, insightful researchers, and skillful teachers.

The final point is that this set of criteria accurately expresses what I think is most important for the students to learn from this experience. What do I care about as your teacher? Look at the variables that contribute to your grade in this class. They express what I care most about your learning from this experience.

Speaking to colleagues in higher education, I ask from time to time whether they would feel comfortable if their own values regarding their disciplines were inferred only from the formal assessments that their students performed. In other words, if a stranger knew you only on the basis of a review of your methods of student assessment, would that person have an accurate picture of what you care most about or what you think is most interesting in your discipline? Many of my colleagues haven't thought much about this question, but upon reflection, they have expressed to me that the means by which they assess their students often is only remotely related to what they care about most or what they find most interesting.

The rationales offered for this disconnect between what teachers value and what they assess often involve extended discussions about having to "cover" certain information or repertoire so that students are "exposed" to the basic components of the discipline. These rationales do not hold up under the scrutiny that questions breadth versus depth. Although you may be able to "cover" the information or skills listed in the course description, can students apply the information and skills in ways that are useful beyond the course? Is the basis of your assessments of student performance their ability to remember and reproduce what they've been told or shown, or does it involve their using what they know and are able to do to solve novel problems and perform skills that were not explicitly taught?

Tests teach

Instructional goals are meaningful only insofar as their accomplishment can be demonstrated by a learner. Statements of intention, that "students will learn to appreciate music," or that "students will learn to think creatively," or that "students will learn to use higher order thinking skills," for example, are meaningless without adequate descriptions of what students will do to demonstrate that they "appreciate music," "think creatively," and "use higher order thinking skills." Absent explicit definitions of the standards of evidence required for documenting appreciation, creativity, and higher order thinking, goal statements like the ones above contribute little to quality instruction.

Goal statements that do include explicit descriptions of what students will do to demonstrate that they've accomplished the goals are, in fact, descriptions of assessment criteria. Statements that "students will choose to listen to three different instrumental selections from the repertoire of the Western art music tradition," or that "students will improvise a three-note melody over a 12-bar blues progression, using the tonic, supertonic, and mediant pitches in a comfortable key," or that "students will explain the relationship between Brahms's symphonies and the symphonies of Beethoven," describe both the goals of instruction and the tasks that students will perform to demonstrate their accomplishment of the goals.

Given the fact that in this way of thinking the goals of instruction and the criteria for assessment are essentially one and the same, how should you begin to define what these goals/assessment criteria should be? Our discipline, like all disciplines, comprises innumerable bits of information and countless component skills. What should serve as the guiding principle in sorting through all of the stuff that can be taught under the heading of Music and defining a set of tangible goals and assessment criteria? What shall we require of students to demonstrate that they have learned what we set out to teach? What will we require as evidence that students have learned?

The answer is first to imagine a competent person who demonstrates all of the skills and knowledge that we're intending to teach and then to define with some precision what that person is like. What does she do? What does she know? What attitudes does she convey? This image supplies us with a vision of our students as accomplished learners, as individuals who demonstrate competence in the fundamental aspects of the discipline. A precise description of this vision defines the assessment criteria. How will we evaluate students' knowledge and skills? By having them do the very things that competent professionals do, but with contextual limitations that are appropriately gauged to learners' levels of experience and expertise.

The difficulties surrounding the design and implementation of assessment can be organized around three dichotomies: skills-content, breadth-depth, and frequency-magnitude.

Skills versus content (Doing stuff versus knowing stuff)

Genuine competence in any discipline is fundamentally based on skills: reading skills, listening skills, reasoning skills, communication skills, social skills. Competence is much more than knowing stuff (content); competence entails doing stuff with what you know, using what you know to reason, solve problems, pose questions, play music, read, discuss, write. Thus it is advantageous for us as teachers to think about the assessment of learning not in terms of what students know, but instead in terms of how students use what they know to accomplish goals. We need not worry that by emphasizing skills we'll shortchange the knowing-stuff, because assessment of the knowing-stuff is subsumed within the assessment of doing-stuff. Knowing that written E on the B-flat clarinet sounds concert D, for example, is inert knowledge. Writing a woodwind quintet arrangement of a four measure melody puts this knowledge into action, applying the knowledge of transposition to accomplish the goal of writing for woodwinds. You have to know stuff (e.g., that B-flat clarinet parts sound a whole step lower than written) to do the doing stuff, so by assessing the doing stuff, the knowing stuff is also assessed.

This focus on skills rather than content is a liberating way to think about goals and assessments, because it alleviates concern over covering material. Teachers who feel pressured by time constraints often move quickly through skills and ideas in the interest of getting through what "must be covered," even though such a rapid pace affords students few opportunities to practice and refine skills. But the development of skills requires frequent opportunities to practice applying the skills in a variety of contexts. No practice, no skill development.

Once the decision is made to forgo allegiance to covering the material (getting through the content), then more time may be spent demonstrating, analyzing, practicing, and refining skills (applying the content to accomplish goals). Focusing on skill development rather than content coverage not only reorients teachers' priorities about the use of precious instructional time but also reorients students' perceptions of what's important, what's deserving of their attention and effort, and what it means to be competent.

Most of the intellectual and physical skills we hope our students will acquire through the course of instruction are not context dependent. Our goal is not that students play this here whole step in tune, for example. Our goal is that students play whole steps in tune, irrespective of where they occur in the pieces they play and sing. Our goal is not that students maintain a steady tempo in this here etude. Our goal is that students learn to maintain steady tempos generally. In other words, our goal is not that students will play or sing a given repertoire (content) but that our students will develop the habits of good musicianship (skills). We may approach this goal through any number of exercises, etudes, and pieces, but irrespective of what's being played or sung at the moment, the goals of musicianship—the skills—are unchanging throughout the course of instruction from the first days of producing a tone.

From this point of view the repertoire performed in a music assessment, for example, is not nearly as important as the quality of the performance. Think about what can happen to students' thinking and priorities when there is no credit for performing very difficult repertoire rather poorly. It's not *what* you play or sing, it's *how well* you play or sing. Sloppy Paganini doesn't win over beautiful Handel, because the criteria now focus on the quality of performance: the beauty of tone, accuracy of intonation, rhythmic precision, expressiveness. The assessment emphasizes that it's the demonstration of refined skills that matter, not the difficulty of the context in which the skills are applied.

Depth versus breadth

The same teachers who make the unfortunate decision to base their instructional goals on content coverage rather than on the development of physical or intellectual skills seldom devote sufficient time and attention to any one idea, principle, or skill, that students come to understand it deeply or perform it fluently. In the competition between breadth (coverage) and depth (competence), breadth often wins. I've heard many teachers insist that they "must get through this material by the end of the semester," as if there is some external force directing them to make this regrettable choice. Although I certainly acknowledge the existence of curriculum guides, textbooks, standardized tests, principals, chairmen, area supervisors, deans, and parents, the assertion that one or more of these forces requires that teachers blow through material faster than students can take it in is demonstrably untrue.

Instructional time is a zero-sum game, and increasing the time devoted to any one topic or skill necessarily diminishes the time available for other topics. But it is generally impossible to cover a great deal of material and develop depth of understanding and fluent skills. There is simply insufficient time to do both. When more time is devoted to a few fundamental skills and a few underlying principles of the discipline and students have many opportunities to practice applying these skills and principles in a variety of contexts, increased competence, fluency, and confidence are the results. The breadth versus depth question is no contest at all. Depth trumps breadth every time. If we expect students to come to value excellence, then we must afford them opportunities to cultivate, nurture, and practice excellence. This represents a considerable investment of time and effort. It doesn't come quickly and it doesn't come cheap, but its value is unassailable. We cultivate excellence by expecting students to demonstrate excellence—depth of understanding and fluency of skills—and by providing numerous opportunities for them to do so.

If we expect students to learn to value deep understanding and intellectual and physical fluency, then we should be certain that all assessments, formal and informal, convey that value. If assessments require only that students repeat what they've been told or imitate what they've been shown, it is unlikely that they will learn to value and invest their time, effort, and energy in their own intellectual or physical skills. This is especially true if assessments are designed in ways that set up students to do poorly. If students are performing repertoire at the brink of their current technical capacity, for example, what is the likelihood that they will play beautifully, expressively, artistically? What if instead of deciding a priori that students must play or sing repertoire at a given level of difficulty, we insist that students play or sing only repertoire that can be performed beautifully, expressively, fluently? In the first instance, everyone performs the same repertoire. Some sound wonderful; others stink. In the second instance, everyone performs repertoire that they can perform beautifully. Some play or sing some very difficult pieces; others perform very simple tunes. But *everyone plays and sings beautifully.* And through repeated experiences like this, the habits of competent performance develop, because all students play and sing beautifully repeatedly.

I realize that some may interpret the preceding as my suggesting that we lower our standards in order for all students to succeed. Quite the contrary. I am advocating for very high standards, because, in the second instance I described above, everyone must sing and play beautifully, a goal that is accomplished by limiting what students are permitted to perform to those pieces that they can perform beautifully. Note however that my high standards are based not on difficulty of repertoire but on quality of performance. Although this view of standards seems to me axiomatic, I have heard it articulated by few devotees of the so-called standards movement. Most often when I hear people argue for higher standards, they're arguing for harder tasks. Of course, this is the cheap and easy way to raise standards: make the assessments harder. It's cheap and easy because it doesn't require that you do anything other than make the test more difficult or raise the passing score. It doesn't require that you teach better, spend more time, or invest more money in materials and equipment.

The success of this type of standards raising is predicated on the naïve belief that improving student performance requires only that the consequences of success and failure increase in magnitude, a belief that curiously persists among many of my Republican friends in spite of the glaring failure of states to improve education by simply raising the bar, of which the New York State Regents Exam is only one of many stunning examples. I certainly do not deny that our expectations can greatly influence what students accomplish, but telling a student who's never learned to think linearly that he'll be held back if he can't perform quadratic equations or write a persuasive essay will do little other than create frustration, anxiety, discouragement, resentment, and no small measure of anger. It certainly won't teach him to think linearly, solve equations skillfully, and write lucid and cogent essays. It will take many, well structured, repeated experiences to do that.

Frequency versus magnitude

Perhaps because so many teachers and students have come to view assessment as an onerous big deal, assessments tend to happen infrequently. In some college lecture classes, for example, students' grades are determined only by a mid-term and a final exam, with few experiences taking place during the other 44 class days that resemble the activities the examinations comprise. What's immediately apparent in this extreme way of doing things is that these "grade producing situations," as they're sometimes called in the education jargon, take on considerable weight in the minds of students. These tests become a big deal both because so much is riding on them and because of their infrequency.

To the extent that such grade producing situations as midterms, finals, juries, and auditions motivate students to get with it and study or practice in earnest, they focus students' attention on the content of the assessments, and if the assessments in fact tap the most important and substantive aspects of the discipline, then this heightened attention to what's most important is not a bad thing. Unfortunately, however, many of these assessments fail to tap the most important and substantive aspects of the discipline, while at the same time creating stress and frustration in students who attempt to cram too much stuff into too little time. Of course, this way of learning is antithetical to systematic habit building. In the absence of sufficient opportunities for consistent, productive repetition over time, even the knowledge that may be remembered, the principles understood, or the skills executed for the test will remain "fragile" in the sense that they will not likely persist much beyond the assessment itself. To understand deeply and to think and move fluently requires active, consistent practice.

I recognize that many of my colleagues argue that the consistent practice and steady effort applied toward understanding and skill are the students' responsibility. Our job as teachers is to convey information, to explain, to demonstrate. It's the students' job to study, practice, and make what we tell them a part of what they think and how they behave. This is a very limited view of the teacher's role in the learning process. To teach effectively we must do much more than convey information. Teaching is much more than telling. The heart of teaching isn't the telling part but the systematic structuring of learning experiences (thinking experiences and doing experiences) that guide students through the acquisition and development of intellectual and physical skills. You can't talk someone into competence. You have to *do* someone into competence.

Assessments contribute to this process when they are generally high in frequency and low in magnitude. Frequent assessments provide opportunities for students to practice applying what they know and demonstrating what they can do, providing important information to teachers and students alike, but also regularizing the act of performing the intellectual and physical skills that everyone is working to master. The increased frequency and familiarity with the tasks associated with the assessment—which ideally are the very tasks that embody the most important aspects of the discipline—render assessment just another part of the learning process. No panic. No sweat. This happens all the time.

The increased frequency also reduces the perceived consequences of error, and this is perhaps the greatest contribution that frequent assessment opportunities make to effective instruction. Students' perceptions of the consequences of error are generally out of whack. All of us have observed or experienced bright, capable, mostly well-adjusted human beings go to pieces before our eyes while arguing over a half-point for a partially correct answer—a half-point that doesn't affect their final grade. I realize this is so common as to be considered an inevitable part of schooling, but it's weird. It's very weird. And it illustrates students' and teachers' lack of perspective about assessment and grading. Think about this carefully.

All intelligent, skillful professionals recognize that error is an inevitable, necessary, and even productive part of thinking and learning. It is virtually impossible to develop genuine competence or to accomplish anything important, for that matter, without sometimes making mistakes, pursuing unproductive paths, or misinterpreting data. Making mistakes is an accepted part of learning new things just about everywhere except in school. In school mistakes cost you, because mistakes lower your grade. And the more *in*frequent the assessment opportunities, the more costly the mistakes.

Understand that we're trying to teach students to adopt a very subtle point of view: don't make mistakes if you can avoid them, but accept the fact that mistakes will happen because they are an inevitable part of learning; try not to make mistakes, but it's OK if you do. The difficulty of acquiring this nuanced way of thinking about learning is evidenced by its rarity among our students. To most of them, mistakes are bad, period. This position is reinforced to the extent that being wrong lowers your grade in a consequential way. When we provide few graded assessment opportunities, we build in *disincentives* for students to comfortably recognize their own errors and accept criticism regarding their work. They can't afford to. Doing so would lower their grade. If error is always associated with a consequential diminution of a learner's grade, what intelligent, motivated student would come to accept error as a natural part of the learning process and appreciatively accept our criticism as a welcome bit of new information that will contribute to their intellectual growth and skill development?

Assessment can and should be a regular part of the process of instruction, even to the extent that it becomes indistinguishable from the process of instruction. If we accept the premise that learning requires the active application of knowledge and skills and the complementary premise that assessments should embody the meaningful application of knowledge and skills, then there should be no impediment to making assessment an ongoing part of teaching and learning. We can accomplish this by creating more frequent assessments that are lower in magnitude in the sense that they are less time consuming and in the sense that each contributes little to the final grade. What often deters teachers from scheduling frequent assessments is the erroneous belief that every student has to be evaluated at the same time. They don't. Or that everyone has to do exactly the same thing on the evaluation. They don't. When assessment is woven into the fabric of instruction, the timing of assessments may vary according to the circumstances.

If all of this seems odd to you, it is only because we have become so accustomed to doing things as they've been done for many, many years. One of the greatest impediments to our thinking creatively about assessment, or about any other aspect of teaching and learning, is that we've all gone to school ourselves. And through our school experiences, we've developed habits of thought that do not necessarily lead to our focusing on the core principles of our discipline. This is not unique to music instruction. It pervades public education in every field of study. We often learn disconnected minutiae about math or science or social studies, wondering how anyone could possibly find this stuff interesting.

Teaching well begins with our formulating a vision of students as accomplished, literate, inquisitive, skilled, thinking musicians. If we take the time to describe an accomplished learner with some precision and if that description is sufficiently explicit, then we have defined simultaneously not only the assessment criteria but the goals of instruction and the nature of the daily class activities as well. All in a single stroke.

This way of thinking about assessment shifts the emphasis away from the *activities* that take place in music class and the *repertoire* that is performed in choir, band, or orchestra, and toward the fundamental skills of intelligent, literate, musicianship that all of us intend for our students to learn. The point of our instructional practice is not, after all, to teach students to perform a particular piece or to participate in a given activity. The music repertoire and instructional activities are only the experiences through which we develop knowledge and skills that will be applicable, meaningful, and useful beyond school. It is these life-long musical and intellectual skills that teachers are working hard to develop, because they form the basis of what students will take with them when they leave school.

SEQUENCING INSTRUCTION

When to teach what

Teachers control the extent to which students succeed in every instructional setting. On any given day, a teacher can make any student seem like the most capable, competent learner or the most bumbling, incompetent boob on the planet, according to the sequence of tasks that the teacher asks the learner to do. This responsibility is as daunting as it is inescapable. Plato's description of Socrates' leading one of Meno's young slaves through a series of questions, at the end of which the boy demonstrates that the square of the hypotenuse of a right triangle is equal to the sum of the squares of the other two sides, is a familiar example of a skillful teacher making an uninformed and unskilled learner look good. Most of us have been the beneficiaries of this type of careful guidance at one time or another in our educational past. Most of us can also remember, sometimes quite vividly, an occasion when a less than skillful teacher made a willing and diligent learner look and feel pretty awful.

All of us with teaching experience recall fondly the occasions when we provided skillful guidance to a student or class that culminated in a successful outcome. But we may be less apt to remember counterexamples in which we inadvertently set up students to fail because we did not effectively organize what we were trying to teach. Of course, the difficult part for all of us is to recognize and accept the fact that we are as responsible for our students' failures as we are for their successes. I'm talking not only about success in accomplishing long-term goals, but more immediately in terms of student accomplishment moment to moment during the course of instruction.

All learning of complex knowledge and sophisticated skills must be approached by first learning more limited and simplified versions of what students are eventually intending to master. The nature of the simplifications—the substance and magnitude of each task, the sequence in which the tasks are presented, the speed of presentation, and number of practice opportunities—has everything to do with the success rates of learners. And the way in which complex ideas and skills are broken down into digestible units is entirely within the purview of the teacher.

Of course, the presentation of most any task or idea can be simplified in a number of different ways, and, at first glance, competing methods of simplification may seem more or less equivalent in terms of their appropriateness and effectiveness. But this is not the case. A given complex skill presented in one form may seem to a novice manageable and doable; the very same skill presented in a different way may seem so overwhelmingly complicated as to be impossible to perform or understand. The teacher's challenge is to determine which method of presentation is best suited to the students she is charged to teach.

Much of the art of teaching comprises structuring and presenting sequences of tasks in such a way that students are able to successfully accomplish what they are asked to do moment to moment. In fact, one of the principal variables that distinguishes the teaching of truly expert, artistic teachers is not so much experts' knowledge of *how* to teach, but their ability to reliably identify *what to teach right now*, at each moment in the learning process.

The goal for today

Observe any student playing or singing and, if you are a knowledgeable musician and a skillful observer, you will doubtless identify many aspects of the student's performance that require attention (and varying degrees of modification) if the student is to improve her skills and develop further as a musician. Observing inexperienced performers in particular, you will probably notice so many things that it will be difficult to know where to begin in dealing with the problems and misunderstandings you identify. In situations like this, novice teachers' attention often gravitates to the most conspicuous errors in students' work, and, at first glance, it may seem to you that salience is an altogether appropriate criterion for determining the priority of instructional goals.

Expert teachers set priorities quite differently, however. Experts assess students' performance and formulate decisions about what-to-teach-now on the basis of (1) the importance of each incorrect aspect of the students' work in relation to (2) its potential effect on the students' overall performance and (3) the probability that the students are actually capable of effecting a positive change in the short term. In other words, experts look to identify the most consequential and solvable problems, whose correction will exert the most far-reaching influence on the students' overall performance. This combination of criteria leads to the identification of goals that create substantive, discernible change in the students' capacity and skill in the short term, and have lasting implications for the long term.

What to teach right now

Once a goal has been identified, the next step in planning instruction is to devise a sequence of tasks that will take students incrementally from what they're able to do reliably now and lead them to the accomplishment of the instructional goal. This may seem rather straightforward at first, but it's complicated.

Students' active participation in the instructional tasks set out by the teacher is the very mechanism through which change is accomplished. It's not the talking part (what you do); it's the doing part (what they do) that matters most. Consequently, the relative effectiveness of the task sequence that you design influences the rate of students' success, a fact that has multiple ramifications.

Certainly it seems reasonable that students who are successful in their attempts to do what teachers ask of them will develop more positive attitudes about whatever it is they're learning than will students who are mostly unable to do what they're asked to do. But even more important is the fact that students who practice applying knowledge and skills (mostly) successfully develop productive, positive *habits*. Of course, students who mostly apply knowledge and skills unsuccessfully develop habits, too. They develop unproductive, negative habits.

Recall from our earlier discussions that the development of any sophisticated skill involves thoughts, behaviors, and attitudes, and that habits of thought and behavior develop through consistent, productive repetition over time. Thus, learning sequences that elicit high proportions of correct behavior and effective thinking increase the strength of productive habits. Conversely, learning sequences that elicit high proportions of incorrect behavior and ineffective thinking, because of the resulting inconsistencies in performance, reduce the habit strength of positive, productive behavior and positive, productive thought.

How you choose to simplify complex tasks and ideas—how you break them down into component parts that are understandable by novices—will determine the extent to which students successfully accomplish the long-term goals of instruction. There are six clear, practical principles of simplification that increase the likelihood that the sequence of instruction will culminate in students' thorough understanding and mastery.

Where to begin?

The first principle concerns where to begin in the course of instruction each day. In presenting an individual student or a class with a new behavior, skill, or idea, what is the most appropriate starting place? Even after students have been acquainted with a given skill or idea over a period of time, how should each episode of instruction start? Should we begin where we left off last time?

Review a bit of what went on during the last session and then move ahead?

You've probably heard some of the shopworn adages that speak to this question—statements like "Start from where the student is," which, on its face, seems logical enough. Of course, statements like "Start from where the student is" raise the question of how you as the teacher actually determine where the student is, exactly… today. This becomes even more complicated in the context of group instruction, where "the student" becomes "the class." If all of the students in the class are not in precisely the same place—and they *never* are—which student do you use to gauge the starting place on a given day? Do you start where the more accomplished students are comfortable? What do you do with the students who are beyond the point at which you begin? What do you do about the students who are not able to perform successfully even at the day's starting place? The question of where to start seemed so simple just a minute ago, didn't it?

Start from scratch—every day

Recall again that we are in the business of developing habit strength in students' positive, productive behavior and thinking. And habit strength increases with consistent, productive repetition over time. Recognizing the unhappy consequences of students' thinking and performing in ways that are inconsistent with the habits we're trying to inculcate, we must devise a procedure by which the likelihood of students' doing things correctly is high at all stages in the learning process. This is not to say that errors will not or should not occur. Errors are an inevitable and potentially productive part of any learning procedure, and it is certainly advantageous for students to learn to cope with error— emotionally, intellectually, and physically—if they are to become effective, independent learners. But in selecting and ordering the tasks that students perform as part of a learning sequence, we can systematically control the success rate of individual performance opportunities and maintain high proportions of successful attempts.

Think about this for a moment in relation to your giving instructions to any person, regardless of his level of competence. At any moment, you can assign a task that seems relatively easy and doable or one that seems nearly impossible. For example, you could ask a student who is just learning to play the trumpet to hold the instrument as you have demonstrated (which has a relatively high probability of success) or you could ask the same student to hold the instrument, form an embouchure, take a breath, and play second-line G in the treble clef (which has a relatively low probability of success). You could ask a student new to statistics to explain what will happen to the value of t in the equation below as the magnitude of the difference between X_1 and X_2 increases (which has a high probability of success) or you could ask the same student to explain the t-score (which has a relatively low probability of success).

$$t = \frac{\overline{X}_1 - \overline{X}_2}{\sqrt{\dfrac{s_1^2}{n_1} + \dfrac{s_2^2}{n_2}}}$$

Of course, when you include only very easy and very difficult tasks in your imaginary instructional repertoire, you quickly recognize the extent to which you as the teacher can control students' levels of accomplishment. Your contribution to students' success rates is less obvious when the difficulty levels of successive tasks are not so starkly differentiated. Regardless, it is possible for you to design and organize consecutive tasks that vary only very slightly in difficulty and complexity, and by doing so lead a student or a class through a sequence of learning opportunities that (1) produces mostly correct responses, (2) minimizes errors, and (3) increases the habit strength of positive, productive behavior and thought.

The core of artistic teaching, the part of teaching that many argue cannot be taught, is nested in this very issue, which embodies the characteristics of all artistic behavior that I've discussed earlier: (1) the simultaneous handling of a great deal of information expressed as many individual variables (e.g., clearly observing student behavior); (2) understanding the relative importance and contributions of each and the relationships among them (e.g., noting which aspects of what students say and do are meaningful and important, which are ancillary, and which are trivial); (3) combining the organization of available information with the selection of options from a repertoire of refined and finely tuned skills (e.g., designing a subsequent task that facilitates accurate performance), (4) one or more of which is then executed with precision (e.g., clearly directing students to think effectively and perform successfully).

Now, to answer the question of where to begin: Start from scratch—every day. By that I mean start from the most fundamental aspects of whatever it is you are teaching, and have the students *demonstrate* these fundamentals precisely and consistently before moving to more demanding tasks in which the probability of students' performing correctly is lower. Many readers are asking at this point how it is possible to make any progress if each day's instruction begins in the same place. How can you get anywhere if you start at the beginning every day?

Consider a beginning student on an instrument, for example. On the first day you meet with the student, you may get him into the proper position to play and teach him to produce a tone. You may even have him play a simple three-note melody. Lesson ends. When the student returns for the next lesson, how accurately do you think he will demonstrate all that you had him do in the first lesson? There will be some things, perhaps many things, that are now out of place, incorrect, or simply in need of refinement. If the student begins where you left off at the end of the last lesson, he will inevitably do some things incorrectly, which will require you to fix the problems that you observe.

Think about the consequences of what I've just described. First, the student has demonstrated (practiced) incorrect performance fundamentals in your presence, thus weakening the habit strength of the correct fundamentals and increasing the habit strength of the incorrect fundamentals. Second, you as the teacher are now faced with going back and re-teaching what you taught last time, but now your job is more complicated than it was in the first lesson. In the first lesson, the student had never done any of this before, and you began by introducing a new behavior. Now, the student has begun to learn a behavior that is incompatible with what you are trying to teach him to do; now, learning involves not only re-introducing the good habit, but also extinguishing the bad habit. Third, the sequence of instruction must now move backward (i.e., away from your intended goal for the day) because you must address things that had been taught previously but which, clearly, had not been learned. Fourth, the student recognizes that he failed to accomplish what you had assigned for him to do, your words of encouragement notwithstanding. All four of these results are bad and avoidable.

Consider an alternative second lesson in which you essentially teach the first lesson again, as if the student had not been through the first lesson. I'm not speaking figuratively here; I'm suggesting that you actually teach the first lesson again. Note the differences between this second lesson and the one described above. First, because you are systematically guiding the student through each component of the fundamentals of performance (as you did in the first lesson), the likelihood is high that he will perform each component accurately and successfully. Second, because your instruction and guidance limits the number of incorrect performance trials, each correct performance trial increases the habit strength of the student's fundamental skills with limited interference from intermittent errors. Third, because you begin at the very beginning, and because the student is mostly successful in accomplishing the tasks assigned moment to moment, the sequence of instruction moves forward, toward the culminating goals that you've planned for the day. Fourth, because your instruction carefully sets up the student to perform successfully, aided by the fact that he's been through this before, the student recognizes and takes pleasure in his own accomplishment. Good, good, good.

The point of the two examples above is obvious. Because your goal is to build habit strength, you must address the same principles many, many times with your student. That much is inevitable. You can choose, however, when in each lesson you address these principles. Your choice is whether to address the principles *after* the student has performed unsuccessfully by correcting his errors, or *before* he performs, thereby setting him up to perform successfully and obviating many errors. Irrespective of when you deal with these fundamental aspects of performance—either by setting them up to be correct or by fixing them when they go awry—you will address them frequently, not only during the initial stages of instruction, but throughout the course of study.

I know of no teacher who enjoys lessons that are consumed by pointing out errors in a student's performance—"you forgot this, you missed that, this was late"—identifying repeatedly aspects of playing or singing that have been addressed in the past but obviously have not been practiced correctly and effectively. And I know of no student who enjoys backtracking through skills and ideas that have been addressed before—skills and ideas that the student believes he has learned "well enough," only to discover that the teacher is dissatisfied with his level of accomplishment. What makes this type of repetition a downer for all involved is not the fact that something that had been addressed previously is being repeated. Repeating is fine as long as students are accomplishing something tangible and things are moving forward. It's the *backing up* that's a big drag—not unlike the way you felt in elementary school when you beat your friends to the lunchroom door by bolting from your classroom and running down the hall ("I made it!"), only to be met by the dowager principal who makes you go all the way back to your classroom and "walk back down the hall like a gentleman." But I'm already here! Ugh.

I am often struck by the master classes I observe that are taught by truly stunning expert performers and teachers. Students come prepared to play very sophisticated and demanding repertoire, hoping to come away with a new perspective on pieces that they're working hard to master, only to discover that the artist-teacher they play for wants to talk about how they take a breath, and how their bow moves on the string, the position of their jaw, and the unevenness of their vowels. I've spoken to many master class participants who are disappointed by experiences like this. Having reached such a high level of performance skill, they are somewhat brought down by having to go back and think about such elementary aspects of musicianship. But these experiences point to the essential nature of well-grounded fundamentals, which all professionals recognize as the sine qua non of artistry. If these fundamental performance skills are not soundly in place (they don't call 'em fundamentals for nothing), discussing the interpretive nuances of a challenging phrase seems beside the point.

Small approximations

The second principle to consider in designing a learning sequence (that will take the class forward from what they're able to do well now to some target goal that the teacher has identified) concerns the nature of the tasks themselves and the distances between them. By distance I mean the difference between the intellectual and physical demands of consecutive tasks.

The path from the starting place to the instructional goal may be best conceptualized as a series of successive approximations that incrementally approach the target goal. It is possible to create a hypothetical sequence in which each succeeding approximation adds only a small measure of increasing difficulty or a single new component to each step in the instructional sequence. The path from any starting place to any goal can be divided into smaller and smaller increments, and this is a useful metaphor for thinking about the path from an instructional starting place to an instructional goal.

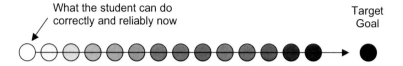

As you are learning to teach, you should practice dividing instructional pathways like this into the smallest increments imaginable, so that between the first, simplest approximation and the final task there are many, many intermediate approximations. This is not to say that every one of these approximations will be included in the instructional sequence that is actually performed in class every day. But it is important that you, the teacher, understand that the path between what students are able to do now and what you intend for them to do (the target goal) may involve any number of incremental approximations.

If our objective is to design an instructional sequence in which most students perform correctly most of the time, the sequence must begin with a task that every individual student in the class can reliably perform successfully. In other words, once the teacher identifies a target, the next question should be What approximation of the target can all of the students in the room perform successfully and reliably *now*? This will be the starting place for the sequence of instruction.

Note that the short-term objective is to perform some approximation of the target correctly first. Why? Again, because we are developing habits of correct behavior and thought. To do that— to increase the likelihood that students will be successful—we must begin with an approximation that has a high probability of success.

After many students have opportunities to *individually demonstrate* this first approximation, it's often beneficial to have them repeat this step in the sequence (correctly) several times—building habit strength. If some students have made persistent errors in the past, there should be multiple opportunities for correct repetitions. In fact, there should be at least as many repetitions of this correct performance as there were incorrect attempts preceding it.

After students perform the first task correctly, then what? How much should be added to the next approximation moving toward the target? How much more difficult or complicated or strenuous should the next performance task be? The answer: no more difficult than the least able students in the class can perform successfully within one to three attempts. If more than a few students are unable to perform a given task successfully after as many as three attempts, then the task (by definition) is too difficult, and the teacher must define a simpler approximation that is closer to what the students can achieve successfully in fewer trials.

After several correct repetitions of the second approximation approaching the target, how much more difficult should the third performance task be? As before, no more difficult than the least able students can perform successfully.

Think carefully about the consequences of such a sequence of component tasks, each of which is incrementally more difficult than the one that precedes it. This type of organization increases the likelihood of successful performance on any given trial, because the new demands that are introduced in each approximation are limited. Each approximation is performed correctly over several repetitions, whereupon a small degree of difficulty or complexity is added in the subsequent task. Thus, the students and the teacher are able to focus their attention on maintaining the quality of performance demonstrated in the preceding trial and correctly performing the new aspect of the current trial.

The advantages of limiting the focus of attention and effort in this way are immediately apparent. This type of sequence builds habit strength because it includes frequent correct repetitions of the component skills of the target goal. It also illuminates the root causes of students' difficulties, because each succeeding approximation involves only an incremental addition of complexity and difficulty.

Consider an alternative sequence in which the third approximation that's attempted, rather than being close to the second approximation, is much more distant, and much closer to the target. The increased difficulty of the more difficult third approximation increases the likelihood that some number of students will be unsuccessful, and repeated unsuccessful attempts will require that the teacher identify the nature of the problem and determine a way to solve it. The nature of the problem may be attributable to any one or more components of the earlier approximations that were "skipped over" between the second and third approximations.

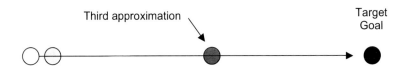

Because some students are unable to do what's being asked of them, the task for the teacher now becomes one of re-simplifying the task (finding a simpler approximation) until the students left behind are able to perform successfully. This backward search through the task sequence may involve many incorrect, unsuccessful attempts, which further weaken the strength of productive habits.

Moving incrementally toward the target goal in the way that I've just described elicits a high number of correct performance trials by permitting both the teacher and the students to focus their attention more clearly on the new aspect(s) of each opportunity to respond. This limited focus of attention increases the probability that the students and the teacher will recognize the students' accuracy not only in terms of the new components of each task, but, equally importantly, in terms of the fundamental aspects of performance that have been introduced previously. The goal, after all, is not merely to perform the new task assigned by the teacher, but to accurately perform the new task while maintaining the integrity of all of the fundamental skills that are basic to quality music making.

Include only essential information

The third principle concerns the amount of information provided to students during the course of instruction. The most effective instructional sequences are elegant in their design. They embody linear presentations of the most important aspects of the skill or idea being taught, with each opportunity to respond systematically approximating the end goal. Elegant sequences include only the information, direction, and modeling that are necessary to elicit successful student behavior—whatever form that may take—and they contain little or no superfluous information that may cloud a clear understanding of purpose or impede progress, regardless of how interesting such information may seem to the teacher.

Often, as I watch teachers attempt to introduce a new skill or idea or change some aspect of an individual student's work, I observe a great deal of talk and demonstration and explanation and elaboration that contributes little to the student's accomplishing what the teacher has in mind. Not that the information that the teachers convey is inherently uninformative; it's just not useful *now*.

And, as I've explained earlier, the decisions of *what* to teach *when* are central to artistic teaching.

All of us who teach have a felt need to explain things to students, but teaching is much more than explaining. Repeating myself again: student learning is not a result of what teachers say, but a result of what teachers have students do.

Let me offer as an example teaching a student in music to use dynamic and rhythmic inflection to create an expressive effect that some might call a "delicate quality." How do you make a phrase sound delicate on the piano? Topics like this often begin with a discussion of the character or emotion that the teacher has in mind (even though the teacher may begin this discussion by posing a series of questions to the student, creating the illusion that the student is coming up with the ideas on his own). Following the discussion and decisions about what the character or emotion should be, the teacher invites the student to create that character or emotion in the target passage in the piece. The student is often unsuccessful, and after a number of unsuccessful repetitions, the teacher tells the student to play a bit softer and separate the notes a bit more, creating a lighter quality. If the student is still unsuccessful (perhaps because he needs even more explicit instructions about what to do physically to create more separation) the teacher may give precise directions about how to play softly and create separation. Following this level of explicitness, the student (finally!) plays softer and with greater separation, producing a lighter quality, and the lesson moves on.

Think carefully about the sequence I just described. The sequence began with a discussion of the intended character of the passage and subsequent attempts by the student to create that character. Of course, the goal is for the student to perform the passage in a way that conveys the intended character. But think about the assumptions embedded in this. The teacher assumes, first, that the student knows what the character sounds like (i.e., the acoustical correlates of the character or emotion described)— in other words, the teacher assumes that, once the student knows what the character should be, he'll have an auditory image of the sounds that connote that character. The teacher also assumes that, even if the student has a good idea about what the character sounds like, he knows what to do physically to create that sound on his instrument. If the teacher's assumptions are well-founded, of course, there's no problem with the sequence of instruction described. But if either of the assumptions is not true (i.e., if the student doesn't know what delicate sounds like, or if the student doesn't know what to do physically to create that sound), the student cannot accomplish the goal that the teacher has set.

Now consider this sequence in reverse. The teacher begins by giving precise instructions about (and perhaps also models to demonstrate) what to do physically to create the intended character on the instrument, which the student then imitates and performs over several repetitions of a brief representative passage. The teacher then calls the student's attention to the sound created, asking the student to describe the acoustical characteristics of the sound and to perform both the old way and the new way and describe the difference in sound that accompanies the different physical motion required for each rendition. The teacher and student then observe and discuss how the sound that results from this physical motion creates an identifiable character or emotional effect in the music.

Note that the second sequence begins with very precise instructions about what to do physically, rather than with a discussion of the resulting character that the student is supposed to create. Because the target is narrowly defined and the instructions are explicit, the likelihood of the student's performing successfully is high. Next, the student has an opportunity to think about and describe a sound that he, himself, has created. The model for discussion is not the teacher's demonstration of delicate, but the student's own performance, which strengthens the pairing of the physical motion with the acoustical result. Finally, the student has an opportunity to think about and discuss the emotional character that this physical-motion-acoustical-result creates.

This last example illustrates the teacher's setting up the student to accomplish a performance goal by beginning the sequence of instruction with very precise directions that lead to the student's performing successfully. The student is successful because of the precision and focus of the instructions. The discussion of the acoustical and musical consequences of the student's performance ensues only after the student has performed successfully.

Over time, as the student acquires greater experience associating physical motions with the sounds that result and the character and emotion they convey, it will become less and less necessary to begin with the precise instructions about what to do physically on the instrument. The student will come to know, through many successful experiences, what delicate sounds like and feels like on the instrument, and will no longer require the explicit instructions that led to his correct performance in the early stages. Now the idea of conveying a delicate character is paired with all of the things that musicians do physically to make a passage sound delicate. And after performing a number of delicate passages that are set up carefully by the teacher, the word delicate in relation to music performance now has a deeper and more extensive meaning. Delicate, a word that once referred only to an abstract concept, is now connected to an auditory image and to physical motion.

Think about the timing of instruction in these examples. All of the same information, instructions, and teacher demonstrations appear in each, but the orders of presentation are entirely different. If the student has no sense of what delicate sounds like and has no idea what to do physically to produce a sound that you or I might describe as delicate, a discussion of the character of the passage is not useful—now. Even if the student comes to state after some prompting and guiding by the teacher that the passage should be delicate, if there's no auditory image of what delicate sounds like or what has to be done by a performer to create such a sound, knowing that the passage should be delicate is not useful, because it suggests no course of action. OK, it should be delicate. So now, how does that sound? Softer? Faster? And once the How does that sound? question has been answered, How do I make the instrument do that?

Of course, this same approach to structuring student experiences applies to intellectual skills as well. Let's consider this same idea in a classroom. When introducing the concept of standard deviation, for example, many teachers begin with a discussion of measures of central tendency, leading up to a presentation of the formula for standard deviation.

$$\sigma = \sqrt{\frac{\sum_{i=1}^{N}(X_i - \overline{X})^2}{N}}$$

Several small data sets are then put up on the screen, and students are invited to calculate the standard deviation of each. Of course, at this point some students generate errors in their calculations ("That's not what I got."), and locating and correcting these errors consume precious class time. Why isn't this a good use of class time now? Because at this point in the learning sequence, calculating standard deviations of hypothetical data sets contributes nothing to students' understanding of the concept of standard deviation. They're just following (or trying to follow) an algorithm to get from here to there (data sets to SDs), having no idea what it is they're doing. Many of those who perform the calculations correctly ("I got it!") in all likelihood don't understand what they're doing either. The problem here is that teachers often mistakenly view this kind of "hands-on" activity as instructive, because students are ... well ... active. But calculating the SDs of the practice data sets is not essential to understanding standard deviation, even though students are actively involved in doing something. Unfortunately, this kind of set up—here's the formula, here are some numbers to practice with, Go!— predicts that many students will make mistakes, and fixing the mistakes in this scenario is as time consuming as it is unhelpful.

Once the calculations have been completed, the errors found, the confusion and frustration abated (sort of), teachers are left to explain how standard deviations are useful in practice and what they mean in statistics. Problem is, many students are still thinking about the calculations, and many more now believe that the most important thing for them to know about standard deviations is how to calculate them.

Consider a different path in which the teacher's discussion of central tendency leads to a problem posed to the class. How do we create a mathematical expression that describes how closely the numbers in a data set cluster around the mean (which puts a problem on the table for which standard deviation is the solution)?

After students have had opportunities to discuss the problem with one another, several students are asked to explain their ideas to the group. The teacher can highlight the more and less effective solutions that are put forward, guiding the students in a discussion of the strengths and weaknesses of each one. Somewhere among the proposed solutions is a suggestion to measure the differences between the individual data points (X) and the mean of all data points $(\overline{X})$ and then calculate an average, an idea that the teacher pursues. Of course, in the process of taking an average of the differences between the individual data points and the mean, someone in the class recognizes that the sum of the difference scores is, and will always be, zero. Hmmm. Now there's a need to perform some transformation that preserves the relationships among the difference scores but solves the problem of their summing to zero, which leads to the suggestion to square the difference scores, thus eliminating the minus signs. Done. Now it is possible to take an average of the squared difference scores: sum the squared difference scores and divide by the number of data points (N). The result is a common statistic, called variance. Now it's possible to unsquare the scores (i.e., take the square root) and get back to the unit of measurement that we started with, leaving an average difference score.

What becomes clear to the students in this procedure is that the standard deviation expresses the average distance between the mean of a distribution and the individual data points in the distribution. It's an average distance from the average. They came to this understanding by approaching the formula as a series of small problems to be solved, each one requiring a creative solution. As a result, the formula for standard deviation is no longer seen simply as an algorithm for "getting the answer." It's an expression of an idea, in which each part of the formula actually means something.

Each step is an approximation of the end goal

The fourth principle concerns the relationship between each performance task in the sequence and the eventual goal that the tasks have been arranged to accomplish. There are many different ways to break down a complicated or difficult skill into its component parts, but not all methods of reduction are equally effective. Most goals can be reached along many different paths, some of which get to the goal efficiently, some of which get there more circuitously, and some of which don't get there at all ("Time's up!"). Designing an advantageous path that is appropriate for the learner and adjusting the elements and direction of that path during the course of instruction are at the heart of artistic teaching.

When we consider any instructional goal, we imagine, almost intuitively, a list of things that a learner would need to know and be able to do to accomplish the goal, recognizing that complicated performance goals usually embody numerous parts that can be identified as distinct elements. And because these elements are intellectually separable, even though they work in concert in the performance of a task, we often plan instruction that addresses these elements one at a time. This way of thinking often leads to our developing a series of prerequisite steps, each of which deals with a different element of the final goal, some of which are quite unlike the ultimate goal itself, and each of which must be accomplished before the final goal is reached.

Activities that may seem, on the surface, to contribute to students' development of component skills may actually be quite inefficient when it comes to applying the component skills in more complicated contexts. Learning efficiency is maximized when all of the elements of the skills are introduced and practiced in contexts that are as much like the final goal as possible. In other words, students learn best when each learning opportunity closely resembles the long-term goal itself.

The challenge for the teacher, then, is to make each step in a learning sequence as close an approximation of the end goal as possible. Of course, it will be necessary from time to time to change the context considerably in order to address serious or persistent problems, but, to the extent that it's possible, each step in a learning sequence should be an approximation of the end goal: the application of the knowledge and skills in context.

Planning often goes astray when the elements that the individual steps comprise are practiced in ways that are unlike the final performance goal—when the contexts in which the elements of the task are introduced and practiced are unlike the context in which they will eventually be employed when the performance goal is reached. For reasons that are entirely understandable, teachers often introduce new ideas and new skills in ways they believe are interesting and engaging to students and that focus students' attention squarely on the ideas or skills being taught. I've observed teachers "teaching breathing," for example, by having students inflate large, plastic bread bags, the ends of which have been taped to empty paper towel tubes, going so far as having students compete with one another in blowing up the bags. The teachers' belief is that this activity will teach students to inhale deeply and fully and to exhale with sustained pressure, important components of wind instrument performance. Although practicing such an activity may in fact increase a student's lung capacity over time, it's important to ask How much is blowing into a plastic bread bag through a paper towel roll like blowing into a trombone? In other words, to what extent does bread-bag blowing approximate trombone blowing? If the answer is Not much, as it is in this case, then it's time to look for other activities that are more like trombone playing that can be used to develop breathing. (Actually playing notes on the trombone comes to mind.)

Consider beginning instruction in bowing as another example. Some pedagogues suggest that bowing instruction begin with activities in which the student manipulates the bow in space away from a stringed instrument. These bow-movement activities are intended to develop bow control that will later be applied to bowing on the strings of a violin or 'cello. And, although practicing moving a bow in space may develop a student's skill in wielding a bow, how much is moving a bow in space like moving a bow on a string? To what extent does bow movement away from an instrument approximate bow movement on a string, taking into account the vectors of motion, the position of the bow in relation to the joints of the arm and shoulder, the pressure required to get a string to vibrate? Is there convincing evidence that this type of "bow practice" is an efficient means of teaching students to move the bow on an instrument?

Remember that the student's challenge in learning the elements of a complex task like music performance is to eventually perform all of the component parts of the task simultaneously *in the context of the task itself* (in these examples, breathing and blowing in the context of trombone playing and bowing in the context of violin playing). So, in planning instruction, the teacher must ask whether it is either necessary or even useful to practice any component of a complex skill in a way that is unlike the skill itself. If we want a beginning trombonist to practice breathing and blowing, is there any better way to practice than by breathing and blowing into a trombone? If we want a beginning violinist to practice bowing, is there any better way to practice than by bowing a string on the violin?

This type of question is important, because it forces us to think about the rationale (and whether there is in fact a rationale) for doing anything in a way that is unlike the goal that we are trying to accomplish. This is not to say that there are no aspects of physical or intellectual skills that can be beneficially rehearsed in contexts that are somewhat removed from the contexts in which the skills will eventually be employed. To the extent that filling up one's lungs with air and exhaling with sustained pressure increases vital lung capacity, even something as seemingly remote as bread-bag blowing can be useful at some level. The question is whether performing this type of activity is the most efficient way to approach the development of the skills of interest. This is a very big issue that pervades instruction in all disciplines.

I use the blowing and bowing examples (and you can think of many more if you take just a minute) to illustrate how activities that may seem, on the surface, to contribute to students' development of component skills may be quite inefficient when it comes to applying the component skills in the context of complex tasks. Learning efficiency is maximized when all of the elements of the performance goal are introduced and practiced in contexts that are as much like the final performance goal as possible. In other words, students learn best when each learning trial closely approximates the performance goal itself. Applying this principle to the breathing and bowing examples just described: wind players learn best about breathing and blowing while they are breathing and blowing into an instrument; string players learn best about bowing when they are bowing strings on an instrument. This may seem overly simplistic, even axiomatic, to some, but many teachers introduce and rehearse elements of complex skills in ways that are quite unlike the contexts in which the component skills will be employed.

Having learners perform tasks that are close approximations of the end goals is important not only in terms of planning instruction, but also in terms of delivering instruction. When students encounter difficulty during the course of an instructional sequence, there is often a temptation to take the student away from the context in which the problem arises and perform one or more remedial tasks in a different, perhaps more isolated, context. Got a problem? Well, I've got just the exercise for you! Belaboring the blowing example a bit, if a student displays some difficulty in sustaining breath on the instrument, the teacher may decide to perform some breathing exercises (off the instrument) to address the problem. The questions raised earlier pertain here as well: Is it necessary or useful to move to a different context to address the problem encountered? Is it possible to deal with the problem effectively in the context in which it first appeared? Rather than have the student begin blowing against his hand or the stand or the wall (or into the bread bag!), is it possible to improve the student's breathing and blowing by modifying the passage that the student is playing, perhaps, but doing whatever needs to be done while actually playing the instrument?

The overarching principle, then, is to make each performance trial in a learning sequence as close an approximation of the end goal as possible. Of course, it will be necessary from time to time to change the context considerably in order to address serious or persistent problems, but to the extent that it's possible, each performance trial in a learning sequence should be an approximation of the performance goal.

Inch forward—leap backward

The fifth principle concerns the movement through the task sequence during the course of instruction. Regardless of the teacher's skill in designing a learning sequence, the difficulty of the steps in any sequence varies from one step to another. All learning experiences are not equally successful, because all tasks are not equally doable and because individual students respond differently to the tasks with which they are confronted. As students progress from one step to the next in a learning sequence, some will inevitably encounter challenges that are so difficult (for any number of reasons) that they cannot overcome them successfully, even after multiple attempts. When this occurs, students who are having difficulty not only fail to accomplish the new task set up by the teacher but also experience a decrement in the quality of previously learned skills that had been performed correctly. What to do now? What should be done when some students, following many attempts, are unable to perform the proximal task assigned by the teacher?

The answer is to leap backward in the sequence to a task that the students who are having difficulty can reliably perform correctly.

Identify a step some distance back in the instructional sequence to a point at which you are confident these students understand what's going on, and begin to approach the problem again from there. Why? Because doing so returns the students to a point in the process that they understand clearly and perform accurately, thus providing an immediate opportunity to refresh the habits of fundamental skills and modes of thought.

Often, when students encounter problems with a given task, teachers do just the opposite of what I've just described: rather than leaping backward in the learning sequence, they *inch* backward, making each task incrementally simpler, but not simplifying things enough so the students who are having difficulty (or are lost entirely) can reorient themselves by practicing ideas they understand. The result is numerous, successive, unsuccessful experiences, during which the weaker students remain confused and inaccurate—bad—and during which the students who get it are becoming frustrated with the need to go back over material they believe no longer warrants their attention—also bad.

Leaping backward to a simplified task that *all* students can deal with effectively is good for a number of reasons. First, students have few opportunities to repeatedly bang up against a wall that elicits unproductive behavior and thought. Instead, when leaping back, they are quickly reminded (not through the teacher's verbalizations but through the students' own behavior) of the successful application of the fundamental principles that have been repeated throughout the sequence of instruction. This is perhaps the most important reason to implement instruction in this way, but there are attitudinal benefits as well. The students whose numbers of unsuccessful experiences are limited enjoy a high proportion of successful experiences that further develop the strength of positive, productive physical and intellectual habits. The students also learn an advantageous procedure for working on their own—a way of approaching problems that permits them to maintain the quality of all aspects of their work while overcoming intellectual or physical obstacles.

Example: A student attempts a given passage with some difficult intervals at tempo, but is unable to negotiate the passage. Teacher asks the student to try it again. Student is unsuccessful. Teacher asks the student to play the passage again "a little slower." The student attempts the passage again and is still unsuccessful. Teacher asks the student to try it again. The student is unsuccessful. The teacher asks the student to try it "one more time" (famous last words). The student is unsuccessful (one more time). The teacher asks the student to play again, but "even slower this time." Again, the student is unsuccessful. The teacher asks the student to play the passage at the slow tempo again but, this time, without playing the written articulation, which the teacher believes is contributing to the student's problem. Again, unsuccessful, but the student lapses into some of the written articulation again. The teacher reminds the student of the instruction about the articulation and asks the student to play again. Even playing all the notes long and connected, the student is still unsuccessful (this is the eighth consecutive unsuccessful trial). The student and the teacher are both becoming a bit frustrated by this time. The teacher asks the student to perform again at the slow tempo, again without the written articulation, but this time only the notes immediately preceding the first difficult interval. Bingo, student is successful (finally!) on this, more limited, task.

As you think about the sequence I just described, consider that each performance trial in which the teacher simplified the task (slower, even slower, all long notes, fewer notes) was an attempt by the teacher to make the proximal goal more doable for the student. Unfortunately, the teacher didn't arrive at a doable task until the ninth performance trial. What was happening during the eight trials preceding the ninth, successful trial? The student was practicing mistakes. Not only were the troublesome intervals being practiced incorrectly, but because the student was focusing much of his limited attention on the problem itself, his attention was drawn away from many of the fundamental components of performance. He became more tense, his position suffered, and his tone quality was poor.

Not only was the student's limited attention directed away from the fundamental components of quality performance in this scenario, the teacher's attention was distracted as well. The teacher was focused on the problem and what may be causing the problem, and less attention was devoted to maintaining the quality of the student's fundamentals. Ever wonder how it's possible that students in a beginning band or orchestra can be sitting with poor posture in February? After all, how hard is it to sit up? How could such a thing happen? Exactly as I've just described. Certainly, the teacher with the bad-posture orchestra had addressed posture in the past, probably many times, but when other problems arose, the teacher's attention went other places, giving students opportunities to practice playing with poor posture without correction, over many, many performance trials. Pretty soon, bad posture is a way of life that is very resistant to change.

What should the teacher have done when the student encountered the passage with the difficult intervals? Well, recall that after two or three unsuccessful trials the teacher attempted to simplify the task for the student by slowing the tempo. Simplification at that point was an appropriate course of action that, unfortunately, did not go far enough. The teacher's decision to simplify what the student was attempting to do was right on target, but the teacher "inched backward" only incrementally, making each task only somewhat less difficult than the one that preceded it. What the teacher should have done after the student's second or third unsuccessful attempt at the passage at tempo as written was to leap backward to what was eventually done only in the ninth trial: slower tempo, even articulation, limited number of notes around one of the troublesome intervals. The teacher and student arrived at that point eventually, but only after eight unsuccessful trials—eight opportunities to practice the passage incorrectly—eight opportunities to lose focus on the fundamental components of quality performance. Bad.

Leaping backward to a simplified task is good for a number of reasons that I've already explained. The student has few opportunities to practice performing incorrectly and is quickly reminded (again, not through the teacher's verbalizations but through the student's own behavior) of all of the aspects of accurate performance fundamentals, which is perhaps the most important reason to implement instruction in this way. The student also learns a way of approaching problems that permits him to maintain the quality of all aspects of his playing while overcoming physical or intellectual obstacles. This is no small thing.

I'm often mystified by teachers who complain about their students' practice inefficiency when those same teachers never do with their students what they expect their students to do on their own, alone in a practice room. The approach to performance problems I've just described is appropriate for both instruction and individual practice, two aspects of music learning that ought not be treated as differently as they often are.

Multiple correct repetitions at each step

The sixth and final principle concerns the importance of repeating correct responses. We often tell students lots of stuff, with the expectation that they're going to do the stuff that we tell them about. Why do we think that, since we have ample evidence to the contrary in our own experiences as teachers and learners? Relying on verbalization as the primary mechanism for developing skills in any domain is almost always unsuccessful. Which is too bad. If you understand something very well and you're in the presence of someone who doesn't, there are few things more pleasurable (if you like to talk and enjoy the sound of your own voice) than explaining what you know. See? Now you understand. Now, you do it (pause) ...... Oh. You can't? Well, let me explain a little more.

As I've discussed previously, this is not an effective course of action. Too much talk. Not enough do. Students don't learn as a result of what teachers tell them. Students learn as a result of what teachers have students do.

Teaching well is like "practicing your students." By that I mean guiding your students through the very activities that approximate and, finally, demonstrate the skills that (you and) they are working to master. Think of your students as instruments that you are practicing and learning to play. What your students do in your presence should be very much like what you hope they will do when they practice on their own. Ever wonder why so many students are so utterly ineffective when they practice? Ask yourself how many times, if ever, they have been guided through a series of activities that exemplify what good practicing is like. The answer is usually seldom or never. Even though they've often been told how to practice, they've never been "practiced" by their teacher. Result: crummy practicing; big drag.

Repetition is the mechanism through which habit strength develops. The more often we repeat a given behavior, the more that behavior becomes a part of what we do. The more often we solve a problem by thinking about it in an effective way, the more likely we are to think about similar problems in similar ways in the future. Although there exists no formula for determining precisely how many repetitions are required before a learner will perform a given operation reliably (i.e., the same way almost every time), it is certainly true that more correct repetitions lead to more successful behavior in the future.

Skill learning is a process of strengthening and reorganizing connections in our heads. Brains are composed of tens of billions of neurons, and throughout our lives, our experiences modify the tens of trillions of connections among them. Everything we do and everything that we experience results in subtle changes in the very structure of the brain.

Skills comprise networks of connections among the areas of the brain that process perception, discrimination, reasoning, and movement. Some of these connections, like the pathways for basic skills like grasping or pointing, are very strong, a result of their having been repeated countless times over a lifetime of experience. Each time we repeat an operation, neural pathways develop among some of the billions of cells in our cerebral cortex, midbrain, and cerebellum, and these pathways facilitate the transmission of electrochemical signals, the physical stuff of thought and action in our heads. The more we repeat something, the more efficient these pathways become and the more we say that something is learned.

The consequences of all of this in relation to developing new habits in students' thinking and doing is obvious: once a student reaches a point that she performs a physical or mental operation correctly, this same operation must be repeated many times before it becomes a somewhat permanent part of the learner's thinking and doing. The longer a student has been performing some aspect of the new operation incorrectly in the past, the more correct repetitions are necessary to weaken the old pathways and strengthen the new ones.

Many teachers teach and many learners practice in ways that ignore this very basic principle of learning. After six or seven unsuccessful attempts to perform a given operation (ugh.), the learner is successful on the eighth attempt (finally!), whereupon he (perhaps even under the guidance of his exasperated teacher) moves on to something else. Seven incorrect repetitions followed by one correct one. Move on. How can this be good? Of course, when it's put this starkly, the problem with a student's performing multiple, consecutive, incorrect repetitions followed by his performing one or two correct repetitions is obvious. But in the context of classes, lessons, and practice sessions, this type of scenario is played out all the time.

This inefficient practice should be replaced with a more successful guiding principle that acknowledges the realities of intellectual and physical development and the building of habit strength: incorrect or unsuccessful attempts at a given operation should be followed by multiple, correct repetitions. How many repetitions? At least as many as there were unsuccessful trials. Observe the practice sessions of experts and you will witness a frequency of correct repetitions that far exceeds the frequency of incorrect repetitions. I don't know whether there is an algorithm for determining precisely how many correct repetitions are required to replace one set of pathways (resulting in unsuccessful performance) with another (resulting in successful performance), but it is clear that the ratio of correct to incorrect trials must far exceed 1.

Often, when teachers get students to a point that they can do something well after numerous failed attempts, the teachers ask the students to "try it one more time," sometimes adding "to make sure it wasn't luck." I encourage you to get the phrase "one more time" out of your repertoire, and replace it with "n more times," n being the some number that is larger than the number of unsuccessful attempts that preceded the first success (e.g., "Let's try this four more times" or "eleven more times" or "twenty-five more times"). Consider how this way of verbalizing and acting will change not only what happens during the course of instruction, but also what happens when the student works on her own. Because a series of unsuccessful attempts in the presence of her teacher is always followed by multiple, correct repetitions, this way of doing things becomes a habit (of behavior and thought), a principle that is much more likely to affect the student's behavior in the practice room than will even the strongest admonition to "repeat things many times correctly when you practice" given in the absence of doing so in the presence of the teacher.

Summary

As you plan and teach, try to incorporate these principles into your thinking and teaching. Start from scratch every day. As you progress through each lesson, make each successive performance task increase in difficulty and complexity only as much as the student can perform successfully in several trials. Include only essential information in the explanations and instructions that you provide to your student. Make certain that each performance task is an approximation of the target goal. When your student encounters persistent difficulty in performing a given task successfully, leap backward in the sequence of tasks to a step that you are confident your student can perform well, demonstrating all of the performance fundamentals that she's mastered up to that point; then, inch forward in approaching the problem skill again. When your student performs a given task correctly following several unsuccessful attempts, have him perform the task correctly repeatedly before moving on to add greater levels of complexity or difficulty.

I realize that this essay is rather dense and contains a lot of information. We'll talk about these issues throughout the remainder of the book, and I hope that as you practice implementing them in your teaching, they will become more and more a part of how you think and that they will lead to your enjoying more successful experiences with your students.

FEEDBACK

How'd I do?

Feedback is perhaps the most misunderstood aspect of teaching, most likely because so much ink has been spilled talking about its meaning and its reputed effects. During the decades when behavioral principles were the dominant force in education, almost everything about teaching and learning was organized around principles of reinforcement and punishment and their effects on student learning and behavior. But much of the information disseminated during that period (and since) comprised either gross distortions of behavior theory or naïve generalizations about behavioral principles. Unfortunately, some of that misinformation has become permanently fixed in the prevailing wisdom in education. Even informal aphorisms about teaching embody many mistaken notions about what feedback is and what it does in the context of teaching and learning.

I hasten to add that the teacher is neither the only source nor the most important source of feedback, even in the classroom. The limited view of feedback as "something that teachers give" is unfortunate because it ignores all of the information that learners acquire from sources other than the teacher. Many teachers operate under erroneous assumptions that teachers are the primary sources of feedback in the classroom or studio and that the effects of feedback are dependent on the teacher's intent. Both of these assumptions are demonstrably false.

I will attempt in this essay to clarify what I believe are persistent misunderstandings about the role of teacher feedback in the learning process and outline several basic principles that underlie the functions of feedback in the teaching of expert practitioners. I divide this discussion into two parts, the first of which concerns feedback in the broad sense—any information that we receive about the consequences of our behavior—and the second of which concerns feedback as it is commonly understood with regard to teaching—information teachers communicate to learners about their work.

Feedback from a broad perspective

Defined most broadly, feedback is any stimulus occurring coincident with or subsequent to a given behavior that a learner associates with the behavior. This definition encompasses the innumerable sources of feedback in our lives, many of which compete for our attention, some of which remain entirely unnoticed, and all of which potentially influence what we do.

Throughout our life experience, we receive feedback nearly all the time. Most of this feedback is not purposeful at all, in the sense that no person or institution has set out to "give us feedback." We do things. And we come to associate certain aspects of our behavior with certain outcomes. Many of these learned associations are advantageous: we learn to breathe deeply before we sing; we learn to smile at our colleagues, even when we disagree with them; we learn to play f-sharps in the key of G; we learn to pay our bills on time. Other of these associations are disadvantageous or maladaptive: we learn to stop playing when we make a mistake; we learn to avoid speaking with people with whom we've had an unpleasant interaction; we learn to fear trying something unfamiliar; we learn to respond with mild nausea before a public performance; we learn to make self-deprecating comments when we feel insecure; we learn to avoid volunteering when a teacher asks a question in class.

Many of the learned associations between behavior and feedback result from relationships that are explicitly discussed or implicitly understood. A grade on a test paper is clearly related to the student's performance on the test. A student's course grade, at least ostensibly, is related to the extent to which the student met the grade criteria outlined in the course syllabus. A teacher's sending a child to time-out is related to the student's disrupting her neighbors during seatwork. Teachers often explain the relationships between feedback and the behavior to which it pertains in an attempt to emphasize the connection for the learner: "You won the audition because you practiced hard and were well prepared." "You got a C because you incorrectly labeled the retransition in your analysis." "You need to play that again slowly because you are still overshooting the interval."

But many other associations between feedback and behavior are a result of only the temporal proximity of the feedback to the behavior; that is, feedback often becomes associated with a given behavior only because of the timing of the feedback, irrespective of whether the relationship is recognized by the learner. These associations, which are seldom discussed in the literature in education, involve feedback that is nonintentional, nonpurposeful, but, as a result of its temporal proximity, may be every bit as effective in influencing behavior as feedback delivered by design.

A full understanding of feedback and its role in learning requires acknowledgement that the teacher is only one of many sources of feedback and that feedback from the teacher does not necessarily function as the teacher intends. There's stuff called feedback that provides information and influences behavior. There's stuff called feedback that doesn't do much of anything at all. And there's stuff that's not called anything at all that provides information and influences behavior.

A student answers a question aloud in class. The teacher informs the student that her answer is correct. Feedback. The teacher asks a question in class. The students raise their hands to volunteer answers. Feedback (think about it). A student plays a section of a sonata movement he's been working on this month. His teacher, who usually offers many positive comments, says nothing except, "Go on." Feedback. A trombonist practicing alone attempts to play a high b-flat, but takes a shallow breath. The note doesn't speak. Feedback. A student makes a smart-aleck comment in class. Teacher scowls. Classmates laugh. Feedback. Feedback. A health-conscious adult overextends himself by beginning a strenuous jogging regimen. His cardiovascular system won't permit him to make it up the hill he attempts to scale. Feedback. A toddler approaches the kitchen stove and places her hand on the glass window in the oven door. The child's fingertip is burned. Feedback. A performer gives a brilliant recital that she's been working on for months. The audience applauds enthusiastically. Feedback. Her parents flew in from Idaho to hear the recital. Feedback. You get the idea. The point I'm making here is that

Feedback can come from almost anywhere.

Feedback is not solely within the purview of teachers, not even in the classroom. It is not solely within the purview of human beings. We receive feedback from oven doors, from trombones, from video games, from parking meters, and from vending machines. By wagging his tail and smiling when I come home and rub his belly and talk baby talk, my dog has taught me that he likes the rubbing and the baby talk. I like to see him wag his tail and smile (well…it looks like a smile to me), so I rub his belly and do the embarrassing baby-talk thing. My dog isn't wagging his tail because he's trying to teach me anything. He's just doing what dogs do when they like something. And I'm just doing what dog lovers do when they see dogs doing what dogs do when they like something. Which brings me to the second important point about feedback:

The function of feedback is independent of its intent.

The stove isn't trying to teach the child anything, but the child learns nevertheless. The students who raise their hand to volunteer aren't colluding to teach the teacher anything, but the teacher learns nevertheless. The trombone isn't trying to teach the trombonist to take bigger breaths either, but that may be the resulting effect. There are instances in which teachers give feedback and nothing happens. There are other instances in which teachers give feedback that they expect to bring about a given outcome and something entirely unexpected happens. Which brings me to the third important point about feedback:

A given feedback event may function differently for different learners and in different circumstances.

The feedback from the trombone described above may lead some students to take bigger breaths. It may lead others to stop playing the trombone. The feedback from his cardiovascular system may lead the novice health enthusiast to adopt a more systematic regimen. It may lead him to conclude that exercise is not worth the effort.

Potentially, feedback conveys information and feedback influences behavior. That's the easy part. The hard part is understanding that the recipients of feedback do not always receive the message that was sent nor do they always change their behavior in accordance with the intentions of the person giving the feedback.

The corrections on a test paper, rather than conveying information about a more appropriate method for solving the problem posed on the test, may instead convey the message that "You can't do math." Positive comments from a teacher following an inescapably abysmal performance, rather than conveying encouragement, may instead convince the student that "This was so awful that the teacher doesn't even think that I can fix it, so he's trying to spare my feelings" or "This teacher's just clueless." This is not to say that a student receiving feedback from a teacher, a parent, or a peer is going through such ruminations about what the feedback means, but even without the deliberate reflection, the feedback may influence behavior. Which brings me to the fourth important point about feedback:

*The associations between feedback and behavior need not be explicitly
recognized in order to exert an effect on behavior.*

Feedback may profoundly affect what we do and think without
our understanding explicitly that *this* is connected to *that*. In fact,
some have suggested that these rather unconscious connections
between behavior and feedback are at the root of much of the persistent maladaptive behavior that we observe in our students, in
our colleagues and friends, and in ourselves.

As the end of the class period approaches, some students begin
to check their watches and stack their books on their desktops in
preparation for the end of class. They are not attempting to signal
the teacher to wrap it up; they're simply aware of the time and are
getting ready to go. The teacher, observing this behavior, is made
aware of the time and begins to bring the lecture to a close. As
weeks pass, the students begin to associate watch checking and
book stacking with class ending. Why? Because within a given window at the end of the hour, watch checking and book stacking are
consistently followed by class ending, and once that connection is
made, the students learn to expect that watch checking and book
stacking will be followed in short order by class ending. How did
they learn this? The teacher, quite unwittingly, taught it to them.
Utterly unintentionally. Very systematically. Very effectively.

A studio teacher, anxious to correct her student's reading errors,
frequently stops the student when he makes a mistake. After each
stop, the teacher offers productive advice, the student's playing
improves, and the lesson moves on, but throughout the lesson,
performance errors are followed by stop signals from the teacher.
Over time, this feedback becomes closely associated with making
mistakes in performance, and despite the teacher's adamant
commands at other times to "keep going when you make a mistake,"
the student finds it very difficult to do so. How did this happen? The
teacher's instructions are very clear. "If you make a mistake, keep
going." But the teacher's nonverbal feedback during the lesson conveys
a different message: "When you make a mistake, I'll stop you." Due

to the consistency of the stopping, irrespective of the fact that it contravenes the verbal instructions about continuing, the student learns to stop when he makes a mistake. Again, the teacher taught him to do this with very consistent feedback. Play … error … get stopped … Play … error … get stopped. The feedback is unintentional, but it is systematically applied and very effective.

A student struggles to produce a good tone on his trumpet. When he plays alone, it is clear to him and to everyone else that his is the poorest sound in the class. Individual performance opportunities are infrequent, but almost every occasion to play alone shows little evidence of progress and is followed by the teacher's offering a list of suggestions about how to improve and another admonition to practice. Other students in the class are much more successful in accomplishing the short- and long-term performance goals outlined by the teacher. Their names are mentioned frequently and they are often congratulated for their work and accomplishment. After a while, the generally unsuccessful student begins to engage his stand partner in conversation, regaling him with examples of alternative uses for trumpet parts. Each time the teacher notices these interactions, he faces the errant student, makes eye contact, issues a stern correction and moves on. As the frequency of these corrections increases so does the teacher's emotional intensity. What association is forming here? Certainly the teacher is not trying to increase the frequency of the disruptions, quite the reverse, but the disruptions are increasing nevertheless. Consider that the student's behavior is being paired with the full, focused attention of the teacher, its negative tone notwithstanding, a level of concentrated attention that the student seldom sees.

Many observers of this scene are puzzled by the child's tenacity in misbehaving and the ineffectiveness of the teacher's emphatic attempts at correcting the child's misbehavior. But think carefully about the feedback that has become associated with the child's behavior. His attempts to play the trumpet are generally met with failure, and his inability to accomplish what the teacher asks him to do is amplified by the relative success of his classmates. When he plays, he receives negative feedback—some subtle, some obvious—from the teacher, his classmates, and his trumpet. But when his trumpet is transformed into a comedic prop, the feedback changes. Classmates smile, and he can command the teacher's attention at will. Think about it. A lot.

Feedback in teaching

If you were to question teachers about the intended functions of feedback, most would assert that feedback serves two purposes: provide information and motivate behavior. A close examination of the actual effects of feedback reveal the same categories: information and motivation. It is certainly possible to further divide these two categories into numerous, smaller compartments—and *many* authors have done so at considerable length—but this kind of pedantic label-generation is of little benefit. I would be remiss in omitting the fact that my concise description of feedback's purposes and effects has been the source of endless argument in education and human psychology, but I'd rather not delve into all of that here, not merely to avoid a fight, but because most of those arguments are decidedly unhelpful and offer little in the way of prescription for sound teaching practices.

Suffice it to say that the implicit and explicit purposes of feedback in teaching are to inform the learner of the quality or accuracy of her work and to impel her to take action or refrain from certain behavior in the future. When a student answers written questions on a test, for example, the teacher returns the test with marks on it, hoping (perhaps expecting) that the feedback will provide information regarding the accuracy of the student's responses and perhaps also that the feedback, if positive, will serve to reward the student for his diligence in studying for the test or, if negative, will serve to punish the student for not studying enough. The teacher's expectation is that the positive feedback, by reinforcing the student's investment of time and effort in studying, will increase the likelihood that the student will study for the next test.

The complementary explanation is that the negative feedback, by punishing the student's inattention to studying, will increase the likelihood that the student will study for the next test (in order to avoid similar punishment in the future).

According to this type of conceptualization, feedback may vary from simple indications of correctness or accuracy (e.g., "Right"; "Nope"; a check mark beside a written response) to more informative descriptions of the quality of performance (e.g., "The way you ended that last note was beautiful!" "You took too much time with the breath and interrupted the rhythm of the phrase."). Any positive evaluation of a student's behavior, in this definition, is labeled positive feedback. Any negative evaluation is labeled negative feedback, although many in education circles have gone to great lengths to avoid using the label "negative feedback," inventing convoluted euphemisms like "corrective feedback" or "constructive feedback." The reasons for this tortuous language are understandable, but the concern with avoiding straightforward, negative assessments of students' work is misplaced and the concocted terms are decidedly unhelpful.

Note that the labels positive and negative feedback are based on the nature of the assessments and not on their function; that is, the definitions are based on the content of the messages conveyed and not the messages' intended or real effects on subsequent student behavior. This distinction is important, because the effects of positive and negative feedback as defined above are not lawful and may vary widely among students and among circumstances.

Just think for a moment about hearing a teacher say "Good" following a student's performance. The extent to which "Good" affects the attitude or behavior of the student to which the comment is directed varies greatly depending on the student, the student's mood, what the student had just done, the tenor of the relationship between the student and the teacher, who else was in the room at the time, the teacher's vocal inflection, whether the teacher was looking at the student when she said "Good," whether the student was paying attention, and a host of other factors. All of which makes clear the folly of talking about "feedback" as if all things labeled feedback function similarly.

Positive? Negative? How much? When?

There is a widely promulgated view that teachers should give as much positive feedback and as little negative feedback as possible—the higher the proportion of positive feedback statements, the better. Some educational prescriptions for feedback promote the extreme view that the *only* feedback students receive should be positive feedback, and that the frequency of positive feedback from the teacher should be very high.

Avoidance of negative feedback is often espoused with vigor. Negative feedback is… well… negative, after all, and negative things are by definition bad. Right? All of us on at least one occasion have observed a teacher deliver a circumlocutory evaluation of a student's glaringly wrong answer or poor performance, all in an effort to avoid acknowledging what the student, the teacher, the student's peers, and anyone else who happens to be watching, clearly recognize is a wrong answer or a poor performance. Question the teacher about his circumlocution and you often receive a heartfelt explanation about nurturing the student and not discouraging him and providing a positive experience. Huh? Why are we making such a big deal about this? The kid gave the wrong answer. It's no big deal. No, really. It's no big deal. Why can't we just say "No, the second theme actually begins two measures later, at measure 84"? Well, we can say that. We ought to say that.

While the teacher is trying desperately to avoid straightforwardly telling the student he made a mistake, the student is getting the idea that he made a mistake. The student is also getting the idea that all of his classmates realize he's made a mistake. And—think about this—the student is also realizing that the teacher thinks that it's a really big deal that he's made a mistake because, rather than just telling the student and getting on with it, the teacher is spending lots of time and energy apparently trying to spare the student's feelings. Suddenly, everything seems… weird.

Of course, the teacher's intent is to soften the negative feedback by taking the long way around. But the feedback message that many students receive in this situation is that expressing a wrong answer aloud in class elicits some apparent weirdness from the teacher, who seems rather uncomfortable. This often makes the students uncomfortable, with the resulting effect that many students learn to avoid placing themselves in such an uncomfortable position in the future; that is, when the teacher asks a question in class, don't volunteer. If you think my little anecdote sounds overblown, ask yourself what you do in class when the teacher invites someone to volunteer to answer a question. Well.... why *don't* you raise your hand?

Some have suggested that such efforts to avoid negative feedback grew out of longstanding social convention. Others argue that the belief in the ineluctable power of positive feedback to teach and the power of negative feedback to discourage is a vestige of behavioral principles misapplied by those who mistakenly equate positive feedback with reinforcement and negative feedback with punishment. Regardless of its etiology, the simplistic and mistaken notion that positive feedback is inherently good and that negative feedback is inherently bad has done much to limit our understanding of teaching and learning, in music and in other disciplines as well.

The teacher's role

Novice teachers often find it difficult to give effective feedback— by that I mean feedback that conveys meaningful information and influences behavior. The reasons for this difficulty are multifarious, but they stem from the fact that we all come to teaching having already learned a repertoire of personal skills that have served us well in most social settings. Many of us learned from our parents to either "say something nice or don't say anything at all," and in most of our day-to-day social interactions this little aphorism is sound advice.

But instructional settings are quite different. The best friendships are reciprocal. The relationships between teachers and students, or between parents and children, are anything but reciprocal. Teachers and parents have a responsibility to teach, and teaching and parenting both involve telling our students and our children what they'd prefer not to hear and making them aware of issues they'd rather not have to face.

Expert teachers give lots of feedback. That is, expert teachers, throughout a learning sequence, make many evaluative statements concerning the quality of students' performances moment to moment. In learning episodes in which students are working to correct specific performance problems, mean rates of feedback can reach as high as six per minute (one feedback statement every ten seconds). That's a lot. It's important to recognize that rates of feedback are associated with a number of other variables. Consider for example that, in order to give feedback at rates as high as six per minute, there must be at least as many opportunities to give feedback. That means that students must have frequent opportunities to do things for which they can receive feedback.

The teaching of experts is characterized by high rates of both positive and negative feedback. Although the prevailing wisdom in education recommends that feedback be mostly positive, systematic observations of experts demonstrates clearly that their use of feedback is quite different from that prescribed, giving both positive and negative feedback at similarly high rates.

One problem in thinking about feedback as a response to student behavior (e.g., performance) is that it gives the mistaken impression that the decision to give positive, negative, or no feedback is merely a reaction to what the student has done. After a student performs, the teacher can comment on the fact that her posture was excellent, that the shift was out of tune, or both. Although this choice is certainly a part of the teacher's decision making, to think about feedback only after the student has done something is to think about feedback too late.

Expert teachers operate quite differently, even though they may not be able to explain what they're doing. They control the rates of positive and negative feedback, not merely by choosing to point out positive or negative aspects of students' performance, but by directing the tasks students perform so that the quality of performance is predictable. As I discussed in an earlier essay, by selecting the tasks a student performs, a skillful teacher is positioned to make any student as successful or as unsuccessful as the teacher chooses on a given performance trial. This ability to determine the quality of student performance moment to moment thus permits the teacher to determine the feedback that the student receives moment to moment.

I know that many observers who have looked carefully at the positive and negative feedback data for expert teachers marvel at the consistency of the ratio of positive to negative feedback, irrespective of the level of the student or the quality of the student's performance. How can this be? How can a teacher give positive and negative feedback that is accurate and yet maintain consistent rates among such a variety of students and tasks? The answer lies in the teacher's skill in controlling the rate of student accuracy by carefully selecting tasks that move students along a path of progress that is well matched to the students' levels of attention, interest, and skill.

My point is that expert teachers do not give feedback only in response to what students do. Expert teachers set up students to perform successive tasks at a predictable rate of accuracy, which in turn creates opportunities to give positive and negative feedback.

Thus, teachers control feedback not merely by choosing to point out certain aspects of students' behavior and ignoring others, but by *controlling the opportunities to give feedback*. If feedback is understood only as a teacher's responses to what students do, then the feedback options are by definition limited by what students happen to do. If a student performs poorly, then the teacher's opportunities to give positive feedback are limited to identifying something about the student's performance that is not germane to the task at hand.

Skillful teachers, wittingly or not, control the rates of positive and negative feedback by controlling the quality of student performance. Many teachers are ready to argue at this point, "I don't control the quality of the student's performance. I give instructions and I'm left to respond to how the student performs." Wrong (negative feedback; see how easy that was?). By selecting what students do moment to moment, the teacher does in fact control the quality of the student's performance. As I discussed in an earlier essay, by carefully controlling the difficulty level of each successive task in a learning sequence, the teacher determines the rate at which students will succeed in accomplishing those tasks and thus determines the rate at which students receive positive and negative feedback.

Want to give a kid some positive feedback as he's working to improve his rhythmic precision? Don't tell him you like his shoes. Don't tell him you think he's sitting with good posture, even though that may be true. Set him up to perform a task in which he is likely to demonstrate rhythmic precision and thereby create an opportunity for the student to perform accurately and receive positive feedback not only from you, but also from his classmates and, most importantly, from his perception of his own accomplishment.

Timing is everything

So how does one do this? How can a teacher give both positive and negative feedback that functions to modify the skills of learners while at the same time motivating them to remain attentive and work hard? The answer is to provide frequent feedback. Teachers control feedback not only through their own verbalizations, gestures, and expressions, but also by structuring learning experiences that provide frequent opportunities for students to respond. And each of these frequent opportunities to respond is an opportunity to receive feedback—from the teacher, from the instrument, from oneself. This is not a trivial point.

Imagine a video game, for example, in which you could invisibly control the rate at which a player wins and loses. From behind the scenes, unbeknownst to the player, you can alter the difficulty level of the game, increasing or decreasing the player's success rate at will. You can well imagine that from this vantage point, you could elicit a number of different responses from the player. You could lead him to believe that the game is a cakewalk, boring, and not worth his time by letting him win with little effort. You could make him think that the game was impossibly difficult, frustrating, and not worth his time by presenting him with obstacles that require a level of skill beyond the player's current capacity. You could let the game progress unguided by you and allow the player's success rate to vary unsystematically. Or you could carefully observe the player's performance accuracy, emotional responses, and effort expended, and systematically modify the difficulty levels of the tasks with which the player is confronted, allowing numerous successes but also creating numerous, well-timed challenges that are difficult enough that they require the player's best efforts but not so difficult as to be insurmountable. In this last scenario, it would be possible to develop in a player a sense of confidence and self-efficacy (I can do this), an attitude of patience (If I keep working at this, I'll get it), and genuine skill.

Of course, the forgoing description pertains not only to a hypothetical video game. It is the nature of skillful teaching. And what facilitates this skillful arrangement of successes and challenges? Frequent response opportunities. On average, many per minute.

The more frequently students respond, the shorter their responses have to be. A minute of performance time may be consumed by one, minute-long performance trial or by ten, 5-second performance trials. When the student plays ten trials in a minute, there are ten separate opportunities for feedback.

Consider the proximal goals you have for your students during a class or lesson and think about how long a student needs to sing or play before you and she know whether she has accomplished the goal. Think of tone quality, for example. If your immediate goal for your student is that she sing a given phrase with a stronger, richer quality, how many notes do you and she need to hear before you know whether she's doing what you asked of her? It certainly doesn't require that she perform an 8-bar phrase. You probably know after the first two or three notes whether she's doing what she needs to do. (If you're really astute you probably know as she's taking a breath before she sings the first note.) So why have her sing the whole phrase?

There are a number of important negative consequences of her singing the entire phrase. First, she may be unable to focus adequately on the goal that you've defined for her because performing the entire passage requires that she think about things unrelated to the goal (e.g., rhythm, diction, a weird interval). Second, if she does not accomplish what you intended, which you knew after the first three notes, but she sings the entire phrase, each repetition consumes a great deal of precious lesson time. You may ask her to repeat the phrase a second or third time. If she still fails to accomplish the goal you've set for her, you may be reticent to have her sing the phrase again, now that more than a minute is passed and she's received negative feedback for three consecutive trials. Feeling a need to say something positive, you may address some aspect of the student's performance other than tone, but it's doubtful that such a comment will provide encouragement for the task at hand and it certainly will convey no information that will increase the likelihood that she'll solve the problem on the next trial.

Consider an alternative arrangement in which, following your instructions, your student sings only the first motive of the passage—just three notes. If she fails on the first attempt, receives negative feedback, tries again, receives negative feedback, tries again, receives negative feedback and more precise instructions, tries again, receives positive feedback, tries again, receives positive feedback again, tries it again, receives positive feedback again, tries it one more time, receives positive feedback again, and then sings the entire phrase with this same tone, you and she will have accomplished the goal having consumed no more lesson time than in the example above with the 8-bar phrases. Why? Because in the second example there were eight performance opportunities—eight opportunities to receive feedback—in the same span of time it had taken to sing the entire phrase three times with no success.

Well, why not have her try to sing the entire phrase, and if she doesn't produce the tone we're going for, just stop her after a couple of notes? Because rather than responding to her errors after the fact, we're trying to set her up to be successful—to do things correctly—before she begins. Each note you allow her to sing with a poor tone is one more moment of poor-tone practice. By having her sing episodes that are only as long as required to accomplish the goal you've set, you create many opportunities to respond and commensurately many opportunities to give feedback, both positive and negative.

Summary

It's important to consider that purposeful use of feedback to shape the behavior of students is a skill with which most novice teachers have had little practice or experience in day-to-day social interactions. Most of us regard feedback as responses to what others do. "I like that." "I don't like that at all." "Don't ask me to sing that again." But purposeful feedback in the context of teaching is quite different. Rather than a response to what happens, purposeful feedback is the planned consequence of a sequence of events that is highly structured and whose outcome is predictable. Whether you choose to think about it or not, you control the rates and timing of much of the feedback your students receive by controlling the tasks that students perform moment to moment. This is a powerful idea—one that has the potential to change the way you teach and improve the work of your students.

As is true of all aspects of skillful teaching, using feedback effectively requires considerable thought and practice, but the changes that you will observe in your students' progress are worth the time and effort that you invest in thinking about this issue and monitoring your feedback when you teach.

TRANSFER

Applying what we know

All of us, when we encounter any new experience or learn any new idea, bring to bear on the new experience some of the knowledge and skills that we have acquired in the past. Everything "new to us" is colored by our past experiences, and every novel learning experience is affected to some extent by what we already know and what we are able to do. Those of us who learned to ice skate as children are likely to learn to skate on roller blades more easily than will someone who has never been on any kind of skates. Those of us whose native language is English can decipher some Romance languages, even without the benefit of instruction, because of what we know about English grammar and syntax and the similarities among words with common roots. Those of us who can drive a car will have little trouble driving a rental truck, even though we've had no explicit training in truck driving. Alto saxophonists will more likely have an easier time mastering the tenor saxophone than will a trumpet player or even a flutist.

The application of acquired knowledge and skills in situations other than those in which the knowledge and skills were originally learned is called transfer of learning or transfer of training in the education jargon. It has been argued, persuasively I think, that all learning involves transfer—that in all learning experiences, learners are influenced to some extent by previously acquired knowledge and skills, and new learning experiences retroactively influence what is already known. But the extent to which a learner advantageously applies what he already knows in novel situations is affected by a number of variables associated with the learner, the learner's past, and the new tasks with which the learner is confronted.

There are innumerable aphorisms that express the importance of the application of knowledge and skills. Sayings like "Learning is what you're left with when you've forgotten everything you've been taught" convey the idea that what a learner is explicitly taught is not as important as the learner's ability to effectively use the information and skills in the future.

A considerable amount of research in education has attempted to explain the extent to which transfer occurs between different types of experiences. As you might imagine, fields in which skills training is either expensive, dangerous, or both have invested a great deal of time and energy in research about transfer. Those responsible for training pilots who will fly complicated aircraft, soldiers who will operate sophisticated weaponry, and surgeons who will perform laparoscopic microsurgery, for example, are naturally interested in transfer effects, since it is either impractical or impossible to train beginners only in the real-life circumstances in which they will eventually have to function. These learners need opportunities to practice the skills that they are attempting to master in controlled situations in which the consequences of error are minimized. So, for teachers, there is a clear advantage to knowing how successfully a given simulation will prepare the learner for the real thing: flying the plane, firing the weapon, or performing the surgery.

Even in less imminently dangerous circumstances (e.g., solving problems in mathematics), teachers must consider how effectively the experiences they provide for their students will prepare students to function in situations unlike those encountered in school (i.e., in real life). Few people would argue that the purpose of school is to teach children to do well in school. That would be a pretty narrow objective, since, for everyone except those of us who become teachers, school eventually ends and students move on. Most would insist instead that the purpose of school is to prepare students for productive lives beyond school, but many teachers, administrators, and parents operate under the untested assumption that much or all of what is learned in school will inevitably benefit students in life beyond school. We assume a lot about what will be meaningful and useful in the future.

Most people who demonstrate intelligence and capability did not receive explicit instructions about every situation they could possibly encounter. They may have received explicit instruction regarding a few basic principles and the application of those principles in a limited number of contexts that provide illustration and opportunities to practice. But learners inevitably encounter situations subsequent to their education and training that require their applying knowledge in skills in ways that have not been taught explicitly. In order to become independent thinkers and doers, learners must eventually use information and skills in situations in which they have had little or no prior experience.

Yet, there is surprisingly little systematic data about how what is learned in school generalizes to life beyond school. One might expect that the long-term value of what is taught in school has been carefully and systematically evaluated, but unfortunately, this not the case. Educational institutions (including private teachers) often operate on the basis of unproven assumptions about the value of the experiences afforded students, and because teachers understand their own disciplines very well, they can envision the potential usefulness of practically *any* activity associated with their subject matters. If the activities are engaging, interesting, and even fun for students, so much the better. The question of whether the knowledge and skills developed during these activities will transfer to situations beyond school is seldom given much thought.

What makes the issue of transfer such an important part of effective instructional planning is the fact that *transfer is not reliably automatic*; that is, learners who encounter novel situations do not always apply their knowledge and skills in ways that effectively solve problems and accomplish goals. Although in the abstract it may seem reasonable to expect that learners will effectively apply all of what we know and can do at every opportunity, there is ample research, dating back to the beginning of the twentieth century, which demonstrates that we often do not.

Development of mental and physical skills

Our understanding of how learning takes place has changed markedly over the past 100 years, and many aspects of intellectual development and cognitive functioning are still being explored and debated by psychologists. Prior to 1900, the incipient field of psychology viewed the human mind in terms of general mental abilities, or faculties, as they were called at the time. These faculties (e.g., problem solving, memory, perception) were believed to be applicable across a broad range of mental functioning, and amenable to strengthening through exercise, not unlike the way muscles gain strength through systematic use. This is an important point, one with far-reaching implications for education, because it implies that any learning that strengthens the mind thus improves all aspects of cognitive performance. This view represents transfer in the extreme: Learning in any domain develops thinking that, by extension, improves performance in all other domains. Learn to solve geometric proofs, and one becomes a more linear thinker. Learn Latin, and one can more easily learn Romance languages. Learn to play the soprano recorder, and one can more easily learn to play an orchestral instrument.

In many ways, this is a very attractive and optimistic view of the learning process. It implies that all learning is good, because all learning develops the mind generally. A more developed mind, enhanced through mental exercise, is more incisive, flexible, insightful, and useful in meeting the challenges that require skilled thought. Much of educational practice in this country was predicated on this view of mental development. Curricula were assembled to develop mental faculties in the belief that, as a result of mental exercise, students would use their well-developed minds to lead productive lives in diverse endeavors beyond school. Even today, most teachers operate under the implicit assumption that what is taught in school will inevitably serve students in the future; that is, what is taught in school will generalize beyond school.

Around the turn of the previous century, psychologists began to test empirically whether learned knowledge and skills do in fact transfer beyond the contexts in which they are taught, and the results were unequivocally disappointing. Knowledge and skills were much more context-bound than the original theory of mental faculties had predicted. Learning was situated in contexts, and very often the knowledge and skills learned in a given context did not generalize to other contexts. In other words, learners did not use all of their knowledge and skills in advantageous ways when confronted with novel tasks or unfamiliar circumstances. Having learned to solve geometric proofs, for example, students were no more likely to think linearly in solving problems unrelated to geometry. Learning Latin did not increase the rate and facility with which students subsequently learned Spanish or Italian. All of the evidence pointed to the inescapable conclusion that transfer is not reliably automatic and that knowledge and skills learned in one context do not necessarily transfer to other contexts.

This is not to say that knowledge and skills never generalize beyond the contexts in which they are taught, of course. Transfer certainly does occur at some level in innumerable situations in our life experience. Most of us could not function if we were unable to use knowledge in skills in ways that had not been explicitly taught. But transfer is by no means a certainty, and learners often do not apply knowledge and skills in advantageous ways. This fact has obvious implications for teaching. If it is possible, or even likely, that students will not effectively apply the information and skills they acquire through their experiences in school, then much of what is taught in school may be of little value once students move beyond school.

The positive outcome of what may be considered disappointing experimental results is that students can *learn* to generalize information and skills beyond the contexts in which they are taught; that is, students can learn to transfer. This fact was demonstrated as early as 1908 by Judd, who showed that learners taught a fundamental principle could apply that principle in subsequent learning in a way that facilitated their acquisition of a new skill. This very positive result also has important implications for planning instruction. Students may not automatically transfer knowledge and skills in ways that are advantageous, but students can certainly learn to do so, especially if their learning experiences are carefully planned to facilitate appropriate transfer.

But how best to plan learning that accomplishes that? What are the variables that affect the likelihood that transfer will take place— that students will generalize when it's appropriate and beneficial to do so? Is there a way to predict the extent to which learners will generalize knowledge and skills beyond the contexts in which they are initially taught?

Answers to these questions require a basic understanding of the nature of transfer itself. Although the definition of transfer is readily understandable on its face, there are some underlying principles that require further explanation.

The nature of transfer

The prevailing wisdom in cognitive psychology currently holds that transfer occurs through two mechanisms, one of which involves the conscious (mindful, reflective) application of decontextualized principles, and one of which involves the unconscious (automatic, nonreflective) application of habits of behavior. These two pathways both explain the application of knowledge and skills in novel or unfamiliar contexts, but they involve subtly different processes that are important to understand if we are to plan learning experiences that increase the likelihood that students will transfer in the future.

Transfer through habits of behavior

The skills of musicianship comprise both physical and intellectual skills, and most of the skills that musicians acquire are generalizable across a broad range of contexts (e.g., across different repertoire, different instruments, different performance situations). In other words, there are physical habits and principles of music making that are applicable in almost all circumstances in which musicians find themselves, and it is these principles that form the core of what we refer to as musicianship.

Much of music learning involves the development of habits, and most musicians well understand the development of the physical habits associated with music performance. But the notion of habits extends to habits of thought as well. Just as there are physical behaviors and physical responses to stimuli that become habits over time, there are intellectual processes (habits of thought) and emotional responses that also become habits over time. These more or less automatized aspects of behavior share a number of characteristics that help explain how and when they are likely to appear in novel or unfamiliar contexts.

I should point out that many (most?) of the intellectual skills of musicianship are ultimately manifested in the physical skill of performance and are not only present inside the skull. Musicians who learn to transpose, for example, have developed habits of thought that are coupled with physical skills that make it possible to look at printed notation in one key and perform the same pitch relationships in another key, often to the astonishment of peers who are not particularly skilled transposers. Due to the typical demands of their performing lives, many accompanists, hornists, and jazz musicians become particularly adept at the skill of transposition.

But what, exactly, is meant by "the skill of transposition"? The term itself gives the impression that transposition is a monolithic construct—that transposition is one thing. But of course transposition is an idea that comprises many component skills. We may think of transposition as a unitary construct only because the component knowledge and skills of transposing have become so tightly bound together in our thinking. If we try to unpack the idea of transposition and enumerate all of its parts, we come up with an impressive list of component skills (e.g., read notation; play from notation; define interval relationships between keys; identify pitches at given intervals above or below written pitches), each of which has its own set of component skills.

Most of us, especially those skilled in transposition, seldom think about the component skills. We think only of transposition, and the individual component skills are embedded in our thinking in ways that are difficult to explain to another person. Many aspiring musicians, having marveled at a peer or mentor who demonstrates some exceptional skill and having asked for an explanation of how to do it, are frustrated by the seeming inability of the expert to explain her expertise. "I just think in the other key." "My hands just go there." Ugh. When you're trying to learn how to do something, such lack of introspection is no help at all.

Transposition exemplifies the nature of many physical and intellectual habits. And there are a number of characteristics that these habits have in common. Consider first how they are developed. Physical habits—like playing position, shifting accurately without looking at the keyboard, and coordinating embouchure, tongue, air, and trumpet to produce an A above the staff—and intellectual habits—like sightreading, transposing at sight, and varying dynamic inflection to create an expressive phrase—all develop through practice and repetition. This might not seem like much of a revelation at first. After all, who would argue with the fact that building habits is a process of repeating whatever it is we wish to become a habit. But it's not quite that simple.

Building habits requires not only repetition, but consistent, productive repetition over time. If we expect a student to develop fluid, relaxed, efficient motion at the keyboard, then the learner must consistently demonstrate fluid, relaxed, efficient motion at the keyboard. Thus it is the teacher's responsibility to create situations that facilitate the student's using fluid, relaxed, efficient motion at the keyboard. If we expect a student to become an accurate, reliable sight reader, then the learner must consistently demonstrate accuracy in sight reading. Again, it is the teacher's responsibility to create situations that facilitate the student's sight reading accurately.

Note that both keyboard technique and sight reading skill, like transposition, are unitary ideas that comprise many component parts. Keyboard technique involves many separate physical movements. Sight reading involves many distinct intellectual processes. But over time, in the mind of the learner (and often in the mind of the teacher), these component parts become bundled together to form a single idea. Even though, at one time early in the learning process, it may be necessary to consider each of these component parts individually, they eventually become fused in a way that renders them no longer amenable to being thought of separately.

Through consistent, productive repetition over time, the physical and intellectual habits of musicianship become learned to the point that they are somewhat automatic and require less and less conscious thought on the part of the learner. All competent musicians have skills in their repertoire that have been rehearsed to a level of automaticity that requires little effort or thought. For example, when it's time to play, the body and the instrument "go to playing position" without a great deal of thought on the part of the performer. Even though at some time in the past, the same performer had to think carefully about the placement of his feet, the position of his torso and limbs, the placement of the instrument in relation to the body, and the position of the bow on the string. Now, all of that is simply, automatically, playing position.

Transfer through the application of principles

Transfer can also take place through the mindful application of principles. Nearly all of the knowledge we possess can be expressed in terms of principles. The fingerings of instruments, for example, are not arbitrary lists of finger positions and key depressions (although many students may think they are)—instrument fingerings are organized around acoustical principles that govern the frequencies of vibrating strings and air columns.

To understand these principles is to understand fingerings in a way quite unlike that of someone who merely remembers which key depressions produce which notes. To know that fourth-line D is fingered 1st valve on the trumpet is to know a specific relationship between a valve combination and a note name. A performer's being able to play a fourth-line D while reading notation is evidence of a learned association between the printed symbol, the physical actions required to produce the tone, and the sound of D. But to know *why* fourth-line D is fingered 1st valve opens another level of understanding that extends well beyond the simple associative connections among the picture of the note on the page, the movements of the body, and the sound of the note.

A performer who knows that D is fingered 1st valve because the 5th partial of the open trumpet (no valves depressed) is E, and that the 1st valve adds a length of tubing necessary for the air column to produce a harmonic series that is one whole step lower than that produced on the open trumpet, possesses an understanding of fingerings that is connected to other useful information: the third partial of the harmonic series is flat compared to equal temperament and the first valve is built just a little bit longer than is necessary to lower the frequency of the open trumpet by a whole step, and these two factors contribute to the result that fourth-line D is "naturally" flat and requires some adjustment from the performer in order to sound in tune. Whew!

Think of some of the principles at work here. Principle 1: Trumpet valves are constructed in such a way that each valve adds a specific length of tubing to the instrument. Principle 2: To compensate for the fact that using valves in combination produces lengths of tubing that are shorter than would be required to produce notes perfectly in tune, the lengths of individual valves are extended slightly (in other words, valve tubing lengths are adjusted in order to approximate in-tune frequencies when valves are used singly and in combination). Principle 3: Trumpet tones are partials of harmonic series which are based on the fundamental frequencies of each tubing length (valve combination). Principle 4: The frequencies of tones of the harmonic series are not identical to the frequencies of the equal tempered scale, and partials of the harmonic series vary in the extent to which they match the tones of equal temperament. Principle 5: Trumpets are constructed in a way that renders them inherently out of tune with equal temperament, and performers must make adjustments with embouchure, airstream, and valve slides to compensate for the instruments' inherent inaccuracies.

Even though the list of principles above is not comprehensive, it is clear that one who understands the principles has a much deeper understanding of the fingering for D on the trumpet. This deeper understanding not only makes the fingering more memorable, but also connects the fingering for D to other fingerings on the trumpet and to the fingerings of other brass instruments. The principles also provide information that is transferable (generalizable), because the fingering for D is no longer an isolated fact. The fingering for D is merely one example of the application of principles that apply to all other notes on the instrument. Knowing the principles makes the trumpet fingerings more memorable, more understandable, and more generalizable.

I hasten to add that many excellent trumpet players who understand these principles implicitly may never have heard them articulated explicitly. And I am not at all suggesting that the way to communicate these principles to students is to begin with a dissertation about acoustical principles and brass instrument construction (I can't imagine a more effective way to convince someone that they are incapable of learning to play the trumpet). But the *teacher* needs to understand these principles very well. Why, especially if the teacher will not explain these principles to the student (at least not now)? Because the teacher will teach differently if the instruction is guided by these principles. The teacher will structure learning experiences for students that illustrate these principles in a number of different ways, and through the skillful design of instructional experiences, the students themselves will come to understand the principles, even if they are never explicitly articulated.

Consider other examples of the application of principles in music making. Decisions about appropriate tempos and other aspects of performance practice are not based on idiosyncratic instructions dictated by composers, editors, or teachers. There are principles governing how fast music should go, when to take time at the ends of phrases, where to crescendo to create an expressive effect. Again, many of these principles are not articulated explicitly during the course of instruction, but teachers who understand the principles they are trying to convey to their students will teach differently (and more effectively) than will teachers who simply teach their students what to do in each phrase of each piece as if there is no connection between the phrases and the pieces that students learn to perform.

Will transfer occur?

The extent to which learners will transfer knowledge and skills is influenced by both contextual similarity and learners' recognition of the applicability of acquired knowledge and skills. These factors are important in understanding the nature of transfer.

Contextual similarity

It seems not at all surprising that learners are more likely to use knowledge and skills in situations that are similar to those in which the knowledge and skills were originally taught. The more similar the circumstances, the more likely it is that transfer will occur. Because many physical and intellectual aspects of performance in any domain are rehearsed to a point of near automaticity—to a point that they are exercised without deliberate thought—familiar circumstances understandably elicit well-practiced behavior. The converse is also true: the less similar the circumstances, the less likely is transfer.

Consider the performance of scales, for example. Having practiced a scale consistently over a period of time, a musician encounters a passage in a new piece that includes the practiced scale. The greater the contextual similarity between the old, practiced scale and the new scale passage in the piece—in terms of tempo, articulation, dynamics, beginning and ending notes—the easier it will be for the musician to perform the new passage. Conversely, the more the new passage differs from the practiced scale (e.g., different articulation, different tempo, different dynamic inflection, beginning on a note other than tonic), the more difficult it will be to apply the practiced skills to the new passage. If the circumstances are different enough, having thoroughly practiced the scale may even interfere with learning the passage in the new piece.

Recognition of applicability

Even when learners encounter situations that appear unfamiliar on the surface, there may be underlying principles that are similar to those found in circumstances with which learners are already familiar. Situations that may appear different in terms of their surface features may be very much alike at a deeper level. The extent to which transfer will occur is influenced by the extent to which learners recognize the similarity between new, unfamiliar circumstances and circumstances that are well known and deeply understood. Again, it seems entirely reasonable that a learner who recognizes that a new situation is like other situations with which she is already familiar will be better able to apply skills and knowledge than will a learner who fails to recognize the similarity and thus the applicability of her knowledge and skills.

For example, many young pianists learn to play the melody in the right hand more loudly than the accompanying voices in the texture, and this principle of bringing out the melody is practiced in a number of pieces. But as their repertoires expand, these same pianists encounter many pieces in which the melody is somewhere other than the top voice in the right hand.

Those who have come to understand that they have been practicing a principle, which states that the melody voice is generally the loudest voice in the texture, will recognize that this principle applies even when the melody appears somewhere other than in the uppermost voice in the right hand. This understanding will lead to their appropriately voicing a passage in which the melody appears in a lower voice. Failure to recognize the principle and its applicability in circumstances in which the melody appears in an unfamiliar place will require the teacher's having to direct the student when to play which voice louder in each new piece encountered. Transfer requires not only that students understand principles but also that they recognize the applicability of those principles in novel contexts.

Relevance is not a sufficient condition

Although it may seem somewhat paradoxical, the relevance of previously learned knowledge and skills does not ensure that transfer will occur. Relevance is not a sufficient condition for transfer. This is an extremely important consideration for teachers planning instruction, because it forces us to recognize that our own perceptions of what's important and what's relevant (i.e., what's connected to what) are quite unlike our students'.

Precisely because teachers are experts in their respective disciplines, we can see the potential relevance of nearly every learning experience that we may provide. Because we understand our subjects deeply, we recognize an interconnectedness among seemingly disparate ideas that may be utterly imperceptible to novices. This recognition of deep structures and relationships is highly advantageous and leads to our functioning effectively, irrespective of our line of work. It allows experts to use information and skills efficiently and creatively. But it may also lead teachers to believe erroneously that a given learning experience is beneficial to students when in fact it is not.

Some teachers may argue that "all knowledge is potentially useful," and that "even if what we teach students now may seem to be of limited value, this here information and these here skills will *eventually* become useful and valued." After all, if all students are on a trajectory to become experts themselves, then it is true that eventually they will need to know everything about the discipline, right? From this perspective, what could not be useful? Everything is or will be useful.

There are two problems with this way of thinking. First, all students of a discipline will *not* become experts, and that's probably as it should be. Think how unfortunate it would be if the only learners who deserved good instruction were those destined to continue studying until they had received a terminal degree. Second, and more important, the timing of learning has everything to do with the usefulness (and thus the importance) of knowledge and skills. Knowledge and skills must be practiced in order to become part of a learner's ways of thinking and doing. Old adages like "Use it or lose it" are generally quite true. If students are to retain what they learn, then knowledge and skills must be exercised regularly. If students are to make use of what they learn in the future and generalize what they learn beyond the contexts in which they were taught, then students must have many opportunities to apply what they know in a variety of contexts.

Negative transfer

The issue of transfer is further complicated by the fact that transfer is not always a good thing. In many circumstances, learners may generalize across situations in ways that are inappropriate, when knowledge and skills learned in the past actually *interfere* with the acquisition of new knowledge and skills in the present (labeled negative transfer). For example, many wind players who learned in a strict tradition of common practice Western music may find it difficult to learn to play in a jazz style, precisely because they apply previously learned information and skills that make the learning of jazz more difficult. Their automatized performance practices, which are different than those required in jazz music, inhibit their learning of jazz. A student who has spent many years playing consecutive eighth notes rhythmically evenly may find it difficult to perform the same printed symbols with an uneven, swing rhythm, or may find it difficult to articulate in ways that are counter to what has been carefully practiced over thousands of performance trials. Likewise, a recorder player who has played only soprano recorder for many years may find it extremely difficult to switch to alto recorder, because the well-learned soprano fingerings produce pitches on the alto that are a fifth lower than the soprano's.

In the situations described above, the learners initially developed habits of performance (i.e., eighth notes played rhythmically evenly, quarter notes played with longer durations, all-fingers-down in the left hand produces a G) and then encountered situations that required the alteration or abandonment of those habits in order to perform successfully. These examples illustrate how transfer can be negative as well as positive. Generalizing can be beneficial if the habits that transfer from earlier experiences are useful in accomplishing intended goals in the present, but generalizing (inappropriately) can also impede learning when the learned habits do not function successfully in a given context.

Facilitating transfer

Is it possible to teach in a way that increases the likelihood that students will use knowledge and skills beyond the contexts in which they were taught? Is it possible to teach students to transfer? The answer is a resounding yes. Understanding how to accomplish this requires clearly differentiating between two distinctly different objectives: (1) learning knowledge and skills and (2) learning to *apply* knowledge and skills effectively. Most instruction in school focuses on the first objective, but often with little attention given to the second. Students learn a lot of stuff, but may be unable to apply what they learn in meaningful ways in the future. This is true not only in music, but in all disciplines in education. I think that most teachers understand how to accomplish the first goal fairly well, but there are many fewer who understand what is necessary to accomplish the second goal, and even fewer who have the skill to actually do it.

Because the variables that may affect transfer are known, it is certainly possible to structure learning experiences that increase the likelihood of transfer in the future. But doing this requires that teachers think differently about how they organize instruction, especially since teaching students to transfer requires considerably more time and effort than does teaching specific knowledge and skills.

Teaching for transfer begins, not surprisingly, with *well-defined goals*. Teachers must ask themselves in the early stages of planning instruction not only Why is it important for students to learn this? but also Why is it important for students to learn this *now*? As I explained previously, all knowledge and skills are potentially useful at some time in the future. But which knowledge and skills are useful and applicable in the near term? By limiting the content of instruction to knowledge and skills that are useful and meaningful in the present, teachers increase the extent to which what is learned now will be retained and applied in the future. Asking the Why-learn-this-now? question almost invariably limits the amount of stuff that is taught in a class, because at any given time there are many skills, facts, and ideas for which there is not a satisfactory rationale.

Asking and answering Why learn this now? illuminates the nature of our own expertise and how our view of the subject matter differs from our students'. When teachers pose this question, they discover that many topics and skills that seemed (to teachers) critical to students' understanding in fact have little value in the present. Eliminating these less essential topics and skills frees precious time for teaching knowledge and skills for which Why learn this now? prompts a clear rationale.

Also essential to facilitating transfer is *repetition*. Most musicians understand the importance of repetition, because practice is a central part of musicians' lives. Repetition is the mechanism through which habits develop. It is the mechanism through which *all* habits develop, both negative habits and positive habits. But positive habits develop only through consistent, productive repetition over time.

Often overlooked is the fact that habits of thought also develop through repetition, just as physical habits do. Thus, accomplishing instructional goals that involve students' thinking effectively requires many opportunities for students to practice thinking and reasoning.

The contexts in which repetition occurs have everything to do with students' learning to transfer. The more varied the contexts in which students practice the knowledge and skills they are working to master, the greater the likelihood that they will effectively apply these skills in unfamiliar contexts in the future (i.e., the greater the likelihood that they will transfer). *Contextual variety* develops flexibility, because thinking and doing in different contexts provides learners with experiences that illustrate the application of knowledge and skills beyond the limited circumstances in which they are first taught. Learners must experience what it feels like and "thinks like" to use information and skills in varied circumstances.

All of this suggests a redefinition of what it means to learn something. Much of what we learn as part of formal education is presented to us in very limited contexts, and we have few opportunities to practice applying what we know and can do in contexts beyond those in which the knowledge and skills are initially taught. But if the goal of education is that students learn to use knowledge and skills effectively in the future, even in unfamiliar circumstances, then *transfer must be defined as the goal of instruction*. The goal is no longer the acquisition of knowledge and skills but the application of knowledge and skills in situations that have not been taught explicitly. For the developing musician, the goal is no longer to play a given piece beautifully, but to play beautifully (period). For the developing writer, the goal is not to write the paper that's due next Tuesday clearly and concisely, but to write concisely in all instances where it's appropriate to do so. For the developing mathematician, the goal is not to deconstruct a given knotty problem into simpler components to obtain a solution, but to use this strategy effectively in approaching all difficult problems.

Since it is clearly impossible to teach a learner how to function in every situation that she will ever encounter in the future, students must learn not only verbal knowledge (declarative knowledge) and skills (procedural knowledge), but also when and how to apply knowledge and skills in situations that have not been taught explicitly. Sounds challenging, doesn't it? It is very challenging.

EFFECTING CHANGE

What's the point?

The purpose of teaching is to change students. Although that statement may seem a bit stark at first, it is nevertheless undeniably true. Students come to teachers—or are sent to teachers—in the hope that they will learn to do things that they could not do prior to instruction. And since the point of instruction is to bring about change, meaningful observation and analysis of teaching must be organized around the changes that teachers intend to bring about in what students do, say, think, and feel. This simple premise is the basis of the observation procedure that I describe in this essay.

The persistent problems associated with teacher evaluation in music and in other disciplines center on the lack of appropriate dependent measures for student learning that illustrate relationships between what teachers do to what students learn. The impediments to defining appropriate dependent measures include both the inexplicit nature of many instructional goals and the inherent complexities in obtaining reliable measurements of student accomplishment over time. If goals are stated only imprecisely, it is impossible to determine the extent to which they are successfully accomplished. And as changes in behavior are measured over larger and larger time scales, it becomes increasingly difficult to attribute the changes observed to identifiable causes. Because there are so many variables that potentially affect what students learn, it's often difficult to connect long-term changes in student behavior to specific experiences. This is especially true when there are no clear intermediate steps along the path from cluelessness to competence.

But unlike some academic instruction, in which students respond either infrequently or not at all during the course of an instructional presentation, music performance instruction provides numerous assessment opportunities throughout each lesson and rehearsal. Every student performance trial is an opportunity to evaluate the extent to which students have accomplished what the teacher set out for the students to do. If the proximal goal is that we "hear more of the inner parts in this passage," for example, then the subsequent performances of the passage provide ample opportunities to assess students' progress. Can you in fact hear more of the inner parts of the passage? If so, then the students have successfully accomplished the proximal goal. If not, then there is more work to do.

The central dependent measure of teaching effectiveness is the extent to which the changes that teachers intend to make are realized in the behavior of their students. Because teachers identify multiple short-term goals over the course of a given class or rehearsal, the accomplishment of each goal may be assessed during the interval or intervals during which the goal is the focus of attention. This procedure creates numerous assessment opportunities, each of which concerns one or more proximal goals of instruction.

What is the unit of teaching?

Every lesson, class, or rehearsal can be divided into intervals of activity that serve definable functions. There are social exchanges that take place typically at the beginnings and endings of instructional periods. There are discussions of assignments past and future. There are intermittent events that provide "down time" or rest from the intensity of extended durations of effort and concentration.

Many of the performance trials that take place in lessons and rehearsals are not intended to change a student's performance or to modify a student's skills, but serve only as opportunities for repetition, intended to increase the habit strength of the fundamental and idiosyncratic skills required to perform the music being played or sung. These intervals of uninterrupted performance time also serve a diagnostic function during which teachers identify flaws in a student's execution as they occur in the context of a piece or exercise.

These are important parts of the instructional process, but they are not the primary mechanism through which changes are made. Changes in performance come about through the skillful arrangement of performance tasks that are structured by the teacher to facilitate the accomplishment of specific goals. Thus, understanding the process through which changes are made requires first that one recognize the proximal goals that are the focus of the teacher's attention at each moment in the lesson, and second that one identify the teacher and student behaviors that are directed toward the accomplishment of those goals.

The important thing to remember here is that the identification of proximal performance goals is only the *beginning* of the process of implementing change. OK, so we know there's a problem or that something needs to change. Now what? Many teachers leave the now-what part to the students: "You tense up in the upper register. You need to fix that." Thanks, but how do I do that exactly? What a skillful teacher does at this point in the lesson is lead the student through a series of performance trials that culminates with the student's singing the passage without the unwanted tension. The positive change in the student's performance doesn't come about only because of what the teacher *tells* the student but because of *what the teacher has the student do.* Thus, the skill in effecting change resides in the intelligent arrangement of instructions, feedback, and, most importantly, student performance trials that facilitate the accomplishment of proximal goals.

An impediment to our thinking clearly about this up till now is the lack of a useful organizing principle for thinking about effecting change in teaching. To evaluate the effectiveness of teaching from the perspective of "the lesson" or "the class" or "the rehearsal" is to view a picture that is too data-rich to be understood clearly. Looking at the whole of a lesson or class is too broad a focus because it is nearly impossible to discriminate among events of varying importance. To observe from the more limited perspective of the precise content of each verbalization or the apparent meaning of each gesture, for example, is too narrow, because it ignores the connections among related events—the student behavior to which the teacher is responding and hoping to influence.

It is when problems are identified and goals are set that the real work begins—when a teacher must decide what she will do and, more importantly, what she will have the student do to bring about the necessary changes in his performance. All examples of excellent music performance instruction include periods of concentrated attention and effort that are clearly directed toward the accomplishment of specific proximal (near-term) goals. And because each of these intervals has a clear focus, the student performance trials in each interval provide opportunities to assess the extent to which the student accomplished the goal set for that interval.

These intervals are an advantageous unit of analysis for music performance instruction. Precisely because each interval offers an identifiable performance goal and encompasses all of the teacher and student behavior devoted to the accomplishment of that goal, each interval offers an occasion to assess the effectiveness of instruction.

The key to this way of thinking about teaching is the use of proximal performance goals as an organizing principle. Throughout performance instruction, teachers identify a number of specific goals that students are expected to accomplish, and it is possible to identify the time periods during which each performance goal is the focus of attention. Each of these time periods frames the instructional activities that are devoted to the accomplishment of one or more performance goals. I refer to these time periods as *rehearsal frames* and the performance goals as *targets*.

The first figure below illustrates four rehearsal frames during the course of an instructional period. The second figure illustrates a single rehearsal frame.

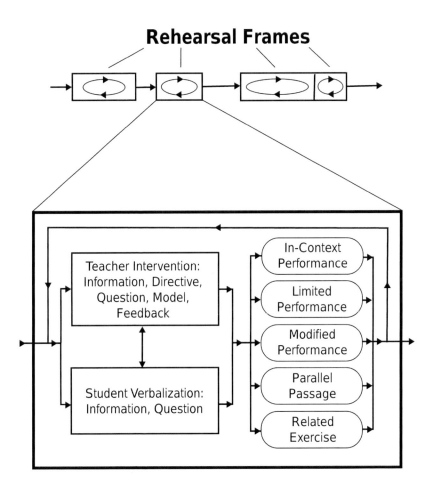

The starting point of each rehearsal frame is defined by the teacher's implicit or explicit identification of a proximal performance goal (target). Explicitly identified targets are relatively easy to observe because the teacher verbalizes precisely what needs to change in the students' performance (e.g., "You must keep the pitch of the C# down."). The teacher may also identify performance goals nonverbally, through modeling (e.g., singing, playing, clapping) or through gestures that indicate what needs to be done. Some targets are not explicitly identified by the teacher, but are inferred from the nature of the tasks assigned to the student. For example, a teacher may ask a student to "play that again more slowly and listen to each note carefully" in an attempt to correct inaccuracies in intonation. Even though intonation is not explicitly cited as the target for the rehearsal frame, the content and sequence of the performance trials are clearly directed toward the issue of intonation.

After a target is identified, the teacher directs the student through one or more performance trials that are intended to effect a positive change in the target. What each performance trial comprises is determined by a number of variables associated with the student, the teacher, the target, the demands of the passage in which the target resides, the salience and importance of the target, and the time required and the time available to accomplish the target. Each of these variables contributes to the teacher's decisions about what deserves attention now, how much attention and effort to expend, and how to approach the target.

I describe below three typical forms of rehearsal frames, any one of which may be an appropriate model of effecting positive changes in student performance. Rehearsal frames come in many configurations. The three I describe below are offered only as a starting point for thinking clearly about the machinery through which change is accomplished.

Form 1—Verbal Directive, One Performance Trial

Often, accomplishing the target requires no more from the teacher than a verbal directive or performance demonstration that calls the student's attention to the target and provides instruction as to how to accomplish the goal. Following the teacher's instructions, the target is performed successfully in the subsequent trial and the lesson or rehearsal proceeds. That the teacher continues without additional repetition of the target passage is an indication that she believes that the change in the target will persist without additional repetition.

In this version of a rehearsal frame, the path through Figure 1 moves left to right through the box in this way: Teacher Directive, In-context Performance, and we're done. This is the least complicated, briefest, and perhaps the most common form of rehearsal frame.

Form 2—Multiple Directives, Multiple Repetitions in Context

The procedure to effect lasting change in student performance often requires more than a single directive and a single performance trial, however. Many rehearsal frames include multiple repetitions of a target passage, all of which are performed in context. In-context performances are those in which the target passage is performed without altering the tempo, the style of articulation, the dynamic inflection, or any other aspect of the passage. Interposed among the multiple repetitions of the target passage are additional teacher directives, modeling, and feedback about the individual student performance trials. Additional repetitions of the target passage are performed until the goal is accomplished and the teacher is confident that the changes in the target will maintain beyond the current rehearsal episode, at which time the lesson or rehearsal proceeds.

In this version of the rehearsal frame, the path through the figure above recycles through several iterations: Teacher Directive/Feedback/ Model, In-context Performance, Teacher Directive/Feedback/Model,

In-context Performance, Teacher Directive/Feedback/Model, In-context Performance, etc., until the target is performed successfully in multiple trials.

Form 3—Multiple Directives, Decontextualization-Modification of the Target Passage, Multiple Repetitions, Recontextualization

Some targets are simply too difficult to be rehearsed effectively in context and must be approached by first decontextualizing the target in a way that facilitates performance accuracy. Repeated unsuccessful performance trials are an indication to the teacher that the disparity between the student's skill level and the task demands of the target passage in context is too great and must be attenuated by modifying the target passage—that is, by defining an approximation of the target passage that is more easily performed successfully in the near term. The approximation (decontextualization) is created by altering one or more aspects of the target passage (e.g., the tempo, instrumentation, dynamics, or articulation).

The capsules on the right in the figure above represent in-context performance and four different levels of performance approximation:

- In-context Performance. The performance of a target passage of at least a full phrase in length with no alterations in any aspect of the performance (i.e., the performance is in tempo and in character).

- Limited Performance. The performance of a target passage that is shorter than a full phrase (e.g., one chord, one measure, one rhythmic figure) but with no alterations in other aspects of the performance.

- Modified Performance. A performance trial in which the target passage is altered beyond simply limiting the amount of music played or sung, including changes in tempo, articulation, dynamics, or instrumentation.

- Parallel Passage. The performance of a passage that appears elsewhere in the music being rehearsed that is similar in content to the target passage.

- Related Exercise. The performance of musical material different from the target passage itself (e.g., scale, arpeggio) that is intended to effect a change in the performance of the target passage.

Once the approximations of the target passage (Limited, Modified, Parallel, Related Exercise) are performed successfully in several consecutive repetitions, the target passage is recontextualized; that is, the target passage is performed as it appears in the context of the piece (i.e., at tempo, as written, in character, and with all expressive inflection). Depending upon the extent to which the target passage was modified, the process of recontextualization may require one or more intermediate approximations leading to the recontexualized performance of the target passage.

These examples illustrate typical rehearsal frames as they appear in music performance instruction. The examples are not arranged in a hierarchy of effectiveness. The content of a given rehearsal frame is not based on an a priori prescription, but is determined by the extent to which students are able to progress toward the accomplishment of the rehearsal frame's goal.

Note again that the organizing principle for each rehearsal frame is the target—the proximal goal toward which the instructional efforts are directed—and the student activities that are intended to accomplish the target. In keeping with the ideas presented in earlier essays, using rehearsal frames as a unit of analysis for teaching and rehearsing focuses attention not on what the teacher says or does but on what the teacher has the students do, and through this lens it is possible to effectively organize systematic observation of teaching and learning for the purposes of both evaluation and prescription.

Observing teaching and learning

There is simply too much that takes place in a typical lesson, class, or rehearsal for an observer, especially an inexperienced observer, to take in all at once and understand with any level of depth. Even if one were to write a description of every verbalization, every performance trial, every movement, every gesture, and every facial expression, this record of observable events would fail to capture the essence of teaching and learning, because such a record would not reflect the timing of events—the *when* and *in-relation-to-what* aspects of teaching.

It has become vividly clear to me, after many years of observing teachers at all levels of expertise, that the differences between competent novices and genuinely expert teachers are not attributable primarily to differences in what they do, but rather, to differences in *when* they do what they do. Novices, experienced teachers, and experts do many of the same things: they often use the same language, the same gestures, the same techniques of instruction. But they differ dramatically in the timing of their behavior in relation to what their students do.

For an observer to recognize the relational-timing aspects of instruction, there must be some organizing principle through which the observer can differentiate what is central, what is ancillary, and what is trivial among the morass of observed events. And in order to accomplish this, there must be some mechanism through which an observer can partition the whole of an observation into manageable intervals that encompass the essential components of teaching and learning. Such an organizing principle must focus on the intended purposes of instruction: the learning goals that teaching is intending to accomplish.

Rehearsal frames provide a unit of analysis for observation and analysis of music instruction that recognizes the heterogeneity of instructional interactions, and because all observation variables are organized around the instructional targets they are intended to facilitate, observation of teaching organized around rehearsal frames permits precise evaluation of the relationships between instructional activities and student achievement. This is possible because achievement is defined according to students' accomplishment of proximal goals, many of which may be addressed during a given period of instruction. Because the targets of instruction are more clearly associated with instructional activities, connections among what teachers do, what teachers have students do, and what students learn are more readily observable than would be the case if attention were directed only to the accomplishment of long term goals.

Using rehearsal frames as a unit of analysis also acknowledges an important point about teaching in general: that within each teacher's experience, even within as brief a time scale as a single lesson or rehearsal, there exists a range of differences with regard to each aspect of the teacher's performance (e.g., feedback, pace, efficiency, effectiveness). The fact that teachers' professional behavior is not monolithic presents both opportunities and challenges for aspiring novices who are looking to capture the important variables that define effective teaching in context.

A TEACHING LIFE

What's love got to do with it?

In public education at the primary and secondary levels, approximately one third of all new teachers leave the field within their first three years on the job. Think about that for a moment. Nearly half of all new teachers are gone after five years. In any given year, most of the teachers who decide to leave the profession have spent fewer than three years teaching. By anyone's assessment, these are dismal statistics.

It may come as a surprise to learn that fewer than 5% of those who leave teaching do so because of the money. After all, most undergraduates and others preparing to teach are smart enough to know from the outset that beginning teachers' salaries are relatively low compared to the salaries of other recent graduates with bachelor's degrees. Prospective teachers also know that teaching is not generally looked upon by others in our society as a prestigious line of work. And they know that teaching requires long hours and difficult schedules, summer breaks notwithstanding.

So why then do so many individuals who invest four (or five or six or more) years earning a teaching degree decide after a very brief time in the field to take a powder and go into business or law or engineering or nursing or something else that has little to do with teaching children? What could motivate them to make such dramatic changes in their life plans after so much personal investment in their own preparation?

The answer is related to the reasons that all of us change our minds about anything in our lives: why we stop reading a book we've started, why we quit a diet plan, why we stop exercising, why we get divorced. The answer, briefly, is this: the reality of our experience does not match our expectations about the experience, and we are unable or unwilling to adjust to the reality of our circumstances. When we begin anything new—a job, a book, a marriage, a diet plan, an exercise program—we have ideas in our mind's eye about what the job, marriage, or diet is going to be like. Some of our ideas are based on direct experience, like doing an internship in the field, reading an excerpt from the book, trying a sample meal, dating, or working out in a fitness club introductory session. Our direct experiences are often somewhat limited, and they may not be directly comparable to the "real thing"—the job day to day, the marriage day to day, reading the whole book, staying on the diet for months or years, exercising regularly.

Some of the data that we consider in formulating expectations may be provided to us by others, in the form of job recruitment seminars, book reviews, friends who offer dating advice, and TV infomercials about *Buns of Steel*. Regardless of the source, these data contribute to our expectations about what life will be like, and the expectations set the bar by which the actual experiences are measured. If the distance between the expectation and the reality is too great, many of us start looking for an escape; some begin looking earlier than others, though others hold on no matter what.

So what is it about teaching that creates most of the dissonance between young teachers' expectations and the realities of their jobs? There are a number of things, as you might imagine: the paperwork (lots), the meetings (boring), preparing for standardized tests (tedious), grading (laborious), dealing with parents who are sometimes unhelpful, or worse (a big pain). But, interestingly, none of these issues is consistently at or near the top of young teachers' lists of Reasons Why I'm Outta Here. What *is* consistently at or near the top of the lists is their inability to motivate and control the behavior of their students. Not all of their students, but some of their students: the "problem students," the ones whose appearance on the absentee list makes the air seem a little fresher and the sun seem a little brighter.

I know that my use of the word "control" may have stepped on a few people's idealism. There aren't many new teachers who state from the outset, "My goal is to control my students' behavior." Instead, they assert that

> I want them to *want* to learn. I want them to be enthusiastic about the subject I'm teaching. I want them to listen and work hard and think and create and express their ideas and follow instructions and cooperate with their classmates and develop skills and contribute to the group and enjoy what they're doing and value the arts and …

All of these are wonderful goals, of course, about which there is a remarkable consensus among teachers, parents, the general public, even politicians. These are goals that all new teachers *expect* to accomplish in their classrooms. They embody the reasons that many of us chose teaching as a career in the first place.

But of course, not all children come to school wanting to learn. Some are not ready to listen or work hard or follow instructions, and they don't enjoy what they're doing, and they couldn't care less about our subject as we present it to them in class. And it is these students who create the dissonance between young teachers' expectations and reality. These students *are* the reality. In fact, all students, at times, do not want to learn and do not listen and do not enjoy what they're doing. The question for us teachers, then, is what do we do about that? What do we do to change the way students behave, to change the way they think? And it is the lack of a satisfactory answer to this last question, combined with a lack of skill, that leads most departing teachers to conclude that tax accounting seems pretty sexy.

Even novice teachers who argue, in the abstract, that they have no desire to "control their students" nevertheless want their students to listen and learn and think and work and enjoy what they do. And if their students don't listen and learn and think and work and enjoy what they do, then they want them to change. Making those changes is what these essays are all about. Positive changes in students' knowledge and skills and attitudes won't come about because of forces outside of our classrooms. Positive changes will happen because of what teachers do to make them happen. This is not to say that parents, administrators, peers, and students themselves don't matter. Of course they matter a great deal. But when students are in our presence it is we who have the potential to create positive experiences that lead to productive changes. Is that hard to do? It's really hard to do.

...*the serenity to accept the things I cannot change...*

Children don't arrive at school like new cars direct from the factory of a single manufacturer. Although they all work in basically the same way, they are far from identical. There are different makes and models, and, just as important, they've all got *lots* of miles on them by the time they get to us. Some have been well cared for, even pampered, and others have been neglected or even abused. Lots more fall somewhere in between. Regardless of their pasts, they've all learned something well before our class begins, and what they've learned creates expectations for what is going to happen and influences their interpretations of, and reactions to, what does happen.

What does this mean for us exactly? How do we accommodate the fact that the students we are charged to teach are so different from one another, at least on the surface? How can we possibly know what to do to reach, guide, and inspire each student when there are so many differences among them and they're all in the room at the same time?

There are several important challenges facing you as a teacher, and the topics of these essays outline what you need to surmount them. Your first challenge is to understand the basic workings of human beings: how the mind works, why we behave the way we do, how we learn. This may seem rather straightforward at first, but it's actually rather complicated. Much of the complication comes from the fact that you've spent the last 21 (or more) years of your lives figuring out on your own the reasoning behind human behavior— your own behavior and the behavior of others. Over the course of your life experience, you've developed intuitive explanations for how people work. Most of you, given the fact that you are socially skilled and generally successful in life, have learned ways of thinking about behavior that function reasonably well within the parameters of the circumstances that you most often find yourselves in.

This is not to say that your skills are errorless or even broadly applicable. Clearly they are not. You sometimes misjudge the character of an acquaintance or even someone whom you consider a friend. You sometimes fail to do things that you know you should, even things you actually want to do. You find the behavior of some people simply mystifying. You are intimidated by car salesmen. Some of you, even now, may find the prospect of facing a room full of 30 or more seemingly enigmatic, unresponsive children a little unnerving.

Nevertheless, you have by now developed a way of understanding behavior that functions at least somewhat positively within your typical life circumstances. But when you venture outside of those circumstances, the rules and explanations that you've worked out over the years sometimes don't apply. When you encounter new or unfamiliar circumstances (like the car salesman), you and others may behave in ways that seem rather inexplicable.

For most of you who are just beginning your careers, teaching classes is outside of your typical experience. You've had little practice organizing, directing, controlling, and evaluating large groups of people, many of whom do not reliably obey the social conventions that you have come to expect of all those with whom you choose to interact on a regular basis. In school, a student may interrupt your lecture, *for no apparent reason!* Another student may refuse to put forth any effort toward completing her assignment. Another may ignore entirely the instructions that you've just spent minutes carefully explaining. Another student begins to cry every time you try to tell him about his work, even when what you tell him is positive. You get the idea. In these circumstances, your intuited explanations of human behavior do not provide adequate information about what's going on, nor do they suggest obvious courses of action that might be taken to improve the situation.

Your second challenge is to understand the mechanisms by which the environment—the physical, intellectual, emotional experiences of life—may affect the workings of individuals. The debate over whether *nature OR nurture* is the prime determinate of human behavior is as old as it is unhelpful. I won't attempt to explain the most recent science related to this issue, but suffice it to say here that it is abundantly clear from a considerable collection of reliable data that both nature (i.e., our genetic endowments and predispositions) and nurture (i.e., the experiences of life) determine who we are (i.e., our behavior). Most important is the extent to which genes and environment *interact* to produce the phenomena we call Luis, Amy, Brian, and Shadonna. Understanding the current thinking on this aspect of human behavior is important, because it permits us to recognize both the limitations of professional interventions and the extent to which specific courses of action may effect positive changes in our students.

...the courage to change the things I can...

Your third big challenge is to master the machinery that creates change in human thinking and behavior—your own and others'. This last challenge is the big one, as it involves not only knowledge but also the skillful *application* of knowledge in the context of teaching. For many of you, the role of teacher is new. You've had little experience making decisions that affect groups of other people, little experience telling others what to do and how to do it, little experience formally evaluating others' work. This is not to say that you've never done any of these things. I'm sure that many of you have, but the tasks before you as teachers require that you apply all of these skills toward the development of students' productive thinking and behaving.

It's not easy to write persuasive prose, or design an ingenious experiment, or deliver a monologue with conviction. It takes a good deal of time and effort and energy to learn to do those things. Many students with whom you'll be working will lack the necessary interest, attentiveness, tenacity, knowledge, or skill to accomplish the goals that you have in mind for them. It is you who then must inspire the interest, foster the tenacity, convey the knowledge, and develop the skill. That's a tall order, one that I hope you find compelling at the same time that you recognize how very daunting your responsibilities will be.

Of course, many of the students whom you teach will arrive with unbridled enthusiasm, incisive minds, boundless energy, or indefatigable motivation. Some lucky few exhibit all of these characteristics. These are the easy ones. These are the students who want very much to learn what you have to teach. It would be nice, I suppose, if classrooms were full of students like that, but they're not, of course. Some students are slower than others; some less interested; others are impatient; still others are easily distracted; and some are just plain unlikable. I could go on, but you can tick off in your imagination the many ways that learners become impediments to their own success much faster than you can read them here.

When you confront these less-than-ready-and-willing students, you must be knowledgeable and skillful enough as a teacher to direct their experiences in ways that overcome the impediments that they bring into the room with them—the lack of knowledge, the negative past experiences, the lack of skill, or the crummy attitude. You can't accomplish this simply by talking to them, although many of you at this point may see talking as the primary mechanism of teaching. No, talking won't do it. Explaining things to them won't do it. Reasoning with them won't do it. It takes much more skill than that.

What will do it is your structuring experiences in your classroom that create opportunities for students to perform successfully in all of the dimensions of their personal and professional (i.e., subject matter related) behavior. That structure encompasses all of the events that take place in your room: what you say, what you demonstrate, what you ask students to do, what you expect from them, how you evaluate their work, how you convey information. But the things that have the most to do with what students learn from you are the things that students actually *do*.

...and the wisdom to know the difference.

Students come with what they come with. You can't change their genetic makeup. You can't change their life histories, including their educational histories. What you can do is order your classroom in such a way as to bring out the very best in the students you teach, applying all of the well-understood and well-documented principles of effective instruction.

It is quite impossible to change directly what someone has in his own head (what someone thinks). It's next to impossible even to *know* what someone has in his own head. It is *very* possible, however, to know what people do—what they say, how they act, how they perform—but even this requires careful observation and precise thinking. It is also possible to *change* what people do by applying your knowledge of the machinery of learning and behavior change—the subject matter of these essays.

I hope that you will channel your enthusiasm and passion for your subject matter and your optimism about teaching into developing the knowledge and skills that are required of effective professionals. Doing so is difficult—as is developing professional level competence in any discipline—but the rewards of skillful teaching, of positively influencing the lives of students, are tremendous.